The
Challenges
of Famine Relief

The Challenges of Famine Relief

Emergency Operations in the Sudan

Francis M. Deng and Larry Minear

THE BROOKINGS INSTITUTION
Washington, D.C.

Copyright © 1992

THE BROOKINGS INSTITUTION

1775 Massachusetts Avenue, N.W.
Washington, D.C. 20036

Library of Congress Cataloging-in-Publication data:
Deng, Francis Mading, 1938–
    The challenges of famine relief: emergency operations in the Sudan / Francis
      M. Deng and Larry Minear.
        p.   cm.
    Includes bibliographical references (p.   ) and index.
    ISBN 0-8157-1792-x (alk. paper) — ISBN 0-8157-1791-1 (pbk.: alk. paper)
    1. Food relief—Sudan.   2. Drought relief—Sudan.   3. Famines—
      Sudan.   4. Droughts—Sudan.   I. Minear, Larry, 1936–
II. Title.
HV696F6D4654   1992   92-22240
363.8'83'09624—dc20   CIP

9 8 7 6 5 4 3 2 1

The paper used in this publication meets the minimum requirements of the
American National Standard for Information Sciences—Permanence of paper for
Printed Library Materials, ANSI Z39.48-1984

Foreword

The international community has become increasingly responsive to humanitarian emergencies throughout the world, whether they result from natural disasters, such as drought, flood, or earthquakes, or from human actions, such as the devastating effect of war on civilian populations. This development may reflect a rising global consciousness, stimulated by better communications. What was remote in the past is now the subject of daily news, dramatized by television coverage. Images of emaciated children or of old women and men who are walking skeletons cannot fail to touch the conscience of those who are more secure and affluent.

In the past, these images tended to be associated with third world countries, especially in Asia and Africa. Increasingly, however, deteriorating environmental conditions, mounting economic difficulties, severe austerity measures, and calamitous ethnic and religious wars are spreading humanitarian crises to massive populations throughout the world. Even the successor states of the former Soviet Union and some countries in Eastern Europe are facing humanitarian tragedies.

As these tragedies and the need for speedy and effective response become recognized as global challenges, it is imperative to learn from the lessons of those countries that have experienced famine and international emergency intervention. This book focuses on the Sudan, geographically the largest country in Africa, which over the last decade has experienced two severe famines caused by drought and civil war. The material contained in the volume originated in studies conducted by the co-authors on these two famines. The study on the drought-induced famine was prepared by Francis Deng for the United Nations Office of Emergency Operations (OEOA) in 1986. The second study, on the war-related famine, was carried out in 1990 by an independent team of African and American researchers headed by Larry Minear, who recaptures in this book parts of the case study.

From these two different cases, the authors contrast the suffering of the masses, especially in the most affected rural areas, with the reticence and denial that characterized the response of the government in Khartoum to both crises. They explain how the international community, initially alerted by the media to the conditions of the Ethiopian refugees in the Sudan, moved in to fill the vacuum with massive relief operations. The cooperation of the Sudanese government with the international community in the war-related emergency proved to be largely successful and is seen as exemplary in the history of emergency operations. The authors conclude by examining the implications of the Sudanese experience for future international humanitarian intervention.

The authors come to their subject from different, but complementary, backgrounds. Francis M. Deng, a senior fellow in the Brookings Foreign Policy Studies program, held a number of posts in the Sudanese foreign service, among them those of ambassador to the United States and minister of state for foreign affairs. Larry Minear, now codirector of the Humanitarianism and War Project, a joint undertaking of the Refugee Policy Group in Washington, D.C., and the Thomas J. Watson Jr. Institute for International Studies at Brown University, has spent many years with nongovernmental organizations on international development and humanitarian issues.

The authors wish to express their deep appreciation to the many people from the Sudanese and international communities who provided them with valuable information through personal consultations. They are particularly grateful to John D. Steinbruner, director of the Foreign Policy Studies program, who urged the authors to prepare materials from their earlier research projects as a book, and made significant suggestions throughout the development of the manuscript. James R. Schneider read an earlier version of the book and offered valuable editorial guidelines. The authors would also like to thank Robert O. Collins of the University of California, Santa Barbara, and Jeffrey Clark, formerly of the Carter Center of Emory University, for reading the manuscript and making useful comments. Because of the unusual nature, diversity, and remoteness of the sources in the research originally conducted outside Brookings, the manuscript has not been subjected to the formal review and verification procedures established for research publications of the Brookings Institution.

Deborah M. Styles edited the manuscript; Gretchen Griener, Kirsten Soule, and Ann M. Ziegler typed many versions of it; and Susan L. Woollen prepared it for typesetting. Lynn Armstrong and Charlotte Shane provided the index.

Brookings gratefully acknowledges the financial support of the Carnegie Corporation of New York, the Rockefeller Foundation, and the Rockefeller Brothers Fund. Brookings also thanks the Red Sea Press for allowing the use of materials from Larry Minear's book *Humanitarianism Under Siege: A Critical Review of Operation Lifeline Sudan.*

The views expressed in this book are those of the authors and should not be ascribed to the people whose assistance is acknowledged above, to the organizations that supported the original studies from which these studies first originated, or to the trustees, officers, and other staff members of the Brookings Institution.

BRUCE K. MAC LAURY
President

July 1992
Washington, D.C.

Dedication

To the memory of the tragic victims of famine who,
neglected, dispossessed, and abandoned by their own
government and leaders, starved to death;

in honor of those who heroically struggled and
survived through their own resourcefulness and
determination to live; and

in gratitude to the international community,
which translated the ideals of global solidarity,
compassion, and generosity into relief operations
that saved countless lives.

May this book be a modest recognition of what
they did and of how it could be done even more
effectively in the future.

Contents

Preface by *Maurice Strong*   xiii

Maps   xix

Glossary   xxii

Introduction   1

1. Famine: Causes and Responses   10
   The Geographic Context   12
   The Demographic Context   13
   The Political Context   16
   Poverty and Underdevelopment   21
   Official Attitudes   24
   Emerging Global Perspectives   29
   The Challenges   32

2. Drought-Induced Famine, 1983–86   38
   Genesis of the Emergency   38
   Intervening from Outside   45
   Framing the Context   50
   Coordinating Activities   54
   Evaluating the Results   66

3. Conflict-Related Famine, 1987–91   83

    Overview of Operation Lifeline Sudan 83

    Intervening from Outside 89

    Framing the Context 97

    Coordinating Activities 104

    Evaluating the Results 111

4. A Look to the Future   120

    The Generic Problems in Perspective 120

    New Horizons on Humanitarian Imperatives 124

    Needed Institutional Reforms 125

    Relief and the Prospects for Peace 130

    Concluding Reflections 134

Appendix A: Persons Consulted for Office of   137
*   Emergency Operations in Africa*
*   Evaluation*

Appendix B: Persons Consulted for Operation Lifeline   139
*   Sudan Study*

Appendix C: Contributing Agencies   145

Notes   147

Selected Bibliography   153

Index   157

Preface

Famines should not occur in a world of plenty. That they do is more a reflection on the continuing imperfections of human society than on the persistent vagaries of nature. This tragic truth was made dramatically evident in the great African famine of 1984–86, which, together with the famine that afflicted the southern Sudan in 1988–91, is the subject of this important and timely book.

My own reflections are based on my experience with the 1984–86 famine, when I served as executive coordinator of the Office for Emergency Operations in Africa (OEOA). The OEOA was hastily established in late 1984 under the direction of Bradford Morse, administrator of the United Nations Development Program (UNDP). At that time attention focused primarily on Ethiopia. Television brought into millions of homes vivid images of Ethiopians suffering and dying from starvation and uprooted from their homes in a land devastated by drought. The world was shocked into an upwelling of compassion and generosity, enabling the mobilization of relief efforts on an unprecedented scale.

In the United Kingdom Bob Geldof and in the United States Harry Belafonte and a galaxy of other stars stirred heartstrings and loosened purse strings. This produced a great outpouring of money and relief supplies. Popular sympathy encouraged governments to support the large-scale international relief operation orchestrated by the United Nations. All this came too late for tens of thousands of Ethiopians who perished before relief could reach them, but it helped many millions more to win their battle for survival.

In the meantime, as world attention focused on Ethiopia, a human tragedy of similar dimensions was quietly unfolding in other parts of Africa, particularly in the Sudan. Here attention centered on the plight of tens of thousands of refugees from the conflict and famine in

Ethiopia who streamed into the Sudan, assembling in improvised camps where relief supplies were available. The Sudanese government of President Nimeiri, while steadfastly ignoring the increasing suffering of its own people, cooperated with international relief efforts in behalf of the Ethiopian refugees. The cooperation created a growing dilemma for the government and for international relief organizations because local Sudanese, themselves suffering from drought and acute food shortages, resented the preferential treatment being given to the refugees in their midst.

This was one of the main problems that I encountered during my first field visit to the Sudan. The water supply had failed at El Fashir in northern Darfur, endangering the 80,000 refugees crowded into the temporary camp there. The provincial governor and the central government, responding to pressure from the local Sudanese, were adamant that no additional camps should be established in the province. I promised the governor that international assistance would be extended to his own people, and he agreed to the establishment of the new campsite. The new camp, however, also required the approval of the central government, and at that time Nimeiri was the government.

I flew to Khartoum to try to persuade Nimeiri. It was not easy. He had strong arguments for not opening new camps; the Sudan was already doing more than its share in accommodating large numbers of refugees, and, while people of the region had been understanding and cooperative, they were now increasingly hostile to the establishment of new camps. I made it clear that I fully appreciated Nimeiri's difficulties, but that the lives of 80,000 people depended on his decision alone, as I had already obtained the agreement of the governor. I implored him on humanitarian grounds to agree, reminding him that the spotlight would focus on this avoidable tragedy. To my great relief he conceded. Knowing, however, that presidential decisions are not always implemented expeditiously, I asked if he would call his secretary and dictate the order immediately. Somewhat taken aback by my request, he nevertheless called in his secretary and dictated and signed the order that spared the lives of 80,000 people.

A few weeks later, I sat in the same office, in the same chair. The occupant of the president's chair was now Abdel Rahman Siwar el-Dahab, the leader of the military government that had just deposed

Nimeiri. Nimeiri's overthrow was at least in part due to the famine he had been so reluctant to confront.

The people afflicted by this famine in the Sudan and elsewhere in Africa were primarily rural people, peasant farmers. They were self-reliant people who in normal times had neither received nor expected aid from their own government or the international community. Only after some seventeen years of below-average rainfall, with their lands dried up and their reserves and resources exhausted, were they forced to leave their homes in order to survive. In the face of unbelievable suffering these people demonstrated qualities of courage, of resourcefulness, and of will that, even more than the international relief effort, enabled them to survive.

If famines bring out the best in some people, they also bring out the worst in some others—merchants hoarding food and charging extortionate prices for it, soldiers and officials appropriating relief supplies for their own use and profit, owners of trucks desperately needed to transport relief supplies doubling and tripling their normal charges. The seeming indifference of some governments to the sufferings and needs of their people is no less shocking.

The famine in the Sudan was a tragedy that did not have to happen. Nature produces droughts; human failings turn them into famines of the kind that Africa has experienced in recent years. It is often said and usually true that rich people do not die of famine. This was certainly the case in the Sudan. Although there were periodic food shortages in Khartoum and in other cities and towns, people in urban areas did not starve. And many of those in rural areas who suffered and starved did so in areas where food was available to those who had the means to buy it.

Persistent poverty and underdevelopment are the real causes of famine. Drought, an important contributing factor, is the trigger that pushes over the edge the poor people who live on the margins of survival. Development is the only solution. Through development peasant farmers can receive the credits, the technical support, and the improved tools and resources they need to diversify and improve their production, the marketing knowledge and support that will increase their incomes, and the roads and other elements of infrastructure that link them with the external economy. Through development they gain access to the education and training, the health care, and the social services that enhance their lives and the prospects for their children and strengthen their own capacities to respond to recurrent emergencies such as drought.

While development is the key to preventing famine, it is also the key to dealing with famine when it occurs. Emergency relief efforts in the Sudan were seriously handicapped by inadequate institutions, both public and private, as well as poor roads and bridges and unreliable and inadequate port facilities, railroads, and communications. The fact that the government of the Sudan was unprepared to respond to a national emergency of this kind compounded these problems and added to the difficulties of overcoming them.

The burdens of moving relief supplies within the country and ensuring their distribution thus fell primarily on the international donor community. The U.S. Agency for International Development and the European Community were particularly active, as were Save the Children, CARE, World Vision, and a number of other nongovernmental organizations. The United Nations undertook the main responsibility for coordinating the efforts of all these actors and for providing support to the government of the Sudan.

On my first visit to the Sudan, in March 1985, I saw that the situation required a leader with substantial experience in emergency relief operations. The Sudanese National Commission for Refugees did not have the leadership, the mandate, or the resources to cope. Although the UNDP resident representative, Arthur Holcombe, was giving exemplary leadership to his agency's development activities, the UNDP and other UN organizations and agencies were geared to carrying out continuing development programs. Brad Morse and I decided that, unlike Ethiopia, where development activities and relief operations had separate leadership, the Sudan called for as close a link as possible between development and relief operations.

Morse chose Winston Prattley, a New Zealander who had extensive experience in relief operations and in development, as the secretary-general's special representative. Prattley's personality contrasted sharply with that of the man he succeeded. Both were competent, dedicated professionals. But whereas Holcombe was quiet and deliberate, the ideal person to preside over UN development activities in normal times, Prattley was ebullient, mercurial, and hard-driving, more disposed to command than to consult. These qualities enabled him to bring a semblance of order to the chaotic situation impeding the relief operation, but they also caused him to step on the toes of some of the officials he had to work with.

Prattley did a remarkable job of putting together under the UN banner an operation that rapidly became the centerpiece for the emergency activities of the international donor community. It provided strong support for the Commission for Relief and Rehabilitation that the Sudanese government set up after Nimeiri's overthrow to replace the ineffective Drought and Desertification Commission. Prattley became a victim of his own success, but as this book makes so clear, in his turbulent period in the Sudan he succeeded in providing the leadership and impetus that turned a confused and chaotic situation into an effective relief operation that enabled hundreds of thousands of Sudanese and Ethiopian refugees to survive the famine of 1985–86.

When I answered Brad Morse's call to join him in establishing the OEOA, I was surprised to learn that the United Nations had no institutional memory of extensive experience with famines and other emergencies. Fortunately, I was able to draw on the experience and guidance of Sir Robert Jackson, one of the truly great men of the United Nations, who generously shared his wisdom and experience as leader of other successful emergency activities. To ensure that the lessons of the African experience were well documented for the guidance of future UN emergency operations, we commissioned independent, in-depth analyses of our experience. One of the authors of this book, Francis Deng, carried out the evaluation for the Sudan.

There is no need here to repeat its conclusions since they are extremely well incorporated, together with the conclusions from the Operation Lifeline Sudan study, into this excellent book: that development is the key to preventing famines, that emergency-response capacity should be an integral part of the development capacities of all countries, and that the ongoing capacity of the UN system to respond to emergencies should be strengthened and the confusion in mandates and responsibilities removed. Most important of all is the need to recognize that preventing these tragedies is far better in both human and economic terms than curing them through hastily mounted relief operations. In the process of saving lives, such operations, by their very nature, can impair long-term development efforts and in some instances undermine the authority and capacities of national and local institutions as often as they reinforce them.

The OEOA, with the help of independent consultants and of the UN organizations and agencies that had been involved in its activities, carried out an evaluation of its experience. Perhaps because it contains some mild criticisms, however, the evaluation was not circulated. Famine and other emergencies continue, unfortunately, and the international community is again focusing its attention on the need for a much greater capacity within the United Nations to respond to them. The experience of the OEOA in the Sudan, Ethiopia, and elsewhere in Africa, as well as that of Lifeline also in the Sudan, may help to enlighten and guide the UN response to future emergencies. This well-researched, authoritative, and timely book will help to ensure that the memory and the lessons of the Sudan famine are not lost. The human tragedy of this famine and the heroic efforts of its victims and those who came to their aid are engraved in my own memory.

MAURICE STRONG

The Sudan

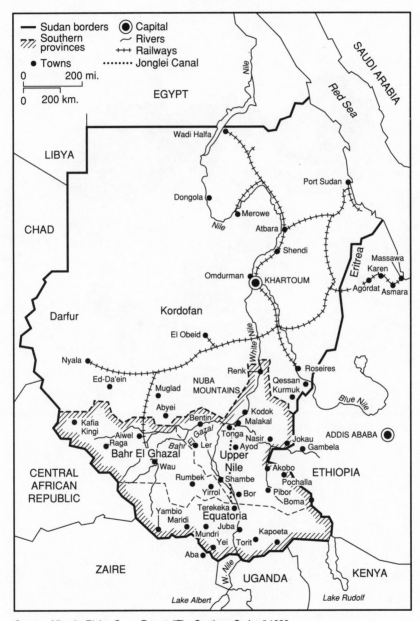

African Emergency Areas

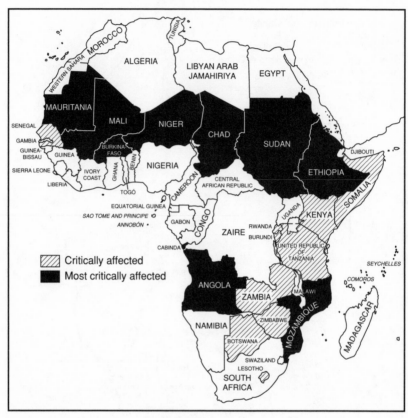

Critically affected
Most critically affected

Source: United Nations Office of Emergency Operations in Africa, 1985.

Operation Lifeline Sudan

Glossary

AID	United States Agency for International Development
FANA	Food Aid National Administration
FAO	United Nations Food and Agriculture Organization
ICRC	International Committee of the Red Cross
LWF	Lutheran World Federation
MALT	Management and Logistics Team (a unit of WFP)
NGO	Nongovernmental organization
OEOA	Office for Emergency Operations in Africa
OEOE	Office for Emergency Operations in Ethiopia
OLS	Operation Lifeline Sudan
RRC	The Sudan Government's Relief and Resettlement Commission
RTO	Road Transport Organization
SPLA	Sudan People's Liberation Army
SPLM	Sudan People's Liberation Movement
SRRA	Sudan Relief and Rehabilitation Association
UN	United Nations
UNDP	United Nations Development Program
UNDRO	United Nations Disaster Relief Office
UNEOS	United Nations Emergency Operation for the Sudan
UNHCR	United Nations High Commission for Refugees
UNICEF	United Nations International Children's Emergency Fund
WFP	United Nations World Food Program
WHO	United Nations World Health Organization

Introduction

With the collapse of ideologies, alliance systems, and governmental structures that divided much of the world for forty years, the international community has acquired both the opportunity for and the burden of creating better arrangements. Traditional objectives of security and economic prosperity can, in principle, be approached in more cooperative ways. Consensus for human rights and human needs can, in principle, be pursued beyond the level of political rhetoric.

The severe economic austerity that has become endemic in many parts of the world makes these aspirations both urgent and difficult. Throughout Eastern Europe and the new states succeeding the Soviet Union, an attempt is under way to create consensual forms of government and market economies at the same time. This effort, requiring a social transformation of unprecedented magnitude, does not as yet command plausibly adequate resources. Economic output in the former communist states is declining from a base that was already too meager to sustain a modern society. That problem is shared, moreover, in many parts of the world with very different political histories.

This situation imposes large demands for the international transfer of resources to mitigate uneven economic development and occasionally to respond to overriding humanitarian concerns. As an international economy slowly forms, so also does a consciousness of international community and acceptance of the ultimate necessity of achieving more widely distributed prosperity. The resources realistically available for assistance are very scarce, however, and their effective application is correspondingly important. As the international community gathers the will to act, knowledge of how to do it becomes a major consideration.

All this makes it particularly important to learn from relevant experience. The period of the cold war overlapped a worldwide process of decolonization. International institutions emerged that are dedicated to providing developmental assistance across sovereign jurisdictions and cultural differences. A record has been accumulated that is full of very instructive lessons, lessons that have been learned at the cost of many failed initiatives but that also enjoy the benefit of some constructive discoveries.

A particularly critical segment of this record concerns experience with providing emergency food relief to populations caught in circumstances of life-threatening famine. Such situations reflect the most extreme breakdown of social order and present the most compelling imperatives for international action. They also make effective action unusually difficult. Though the international community has always had adequate food to prevent mass starvation, distributing it to threatened populations has presented major practical difficulties deriving from the circumstances that cause the famine itself. The individuals at greatest risk are often also the least accessible. The process of giving them vital commodities tempts thieves and weakens indigenous producers. Emergency intervention even for the most compelling of reasons can readily have perverse effects on a society in crisis.

The recent historical record contains ample evidence of such effects, but also guidelines for mitigating them. As the international community faces the formidable and unavoidable task of responding to the needs of Eastern Europe and the former Soviet Union, it must bring accumulated experience to bear. Episodes of emergency famine are clearly possible. Even if unpredictable fortune proves to be less harsh, the experience with emergency relief operations informs the general process of international assistance.

This study focuses on two famine emergencies in the Sudan during the 1980s and the response they generated from inside the country and from the international community. The first famine, triggered by prolonged drought, affected mostly the western and eastern parts of the North during the years 1983–86. The second famine affected mostly the inhabitants of the southern Sudan, where a civil war of great ferocity has been raging intermittently since 1955; it halted in 1972 and broke out again in 1983. The conflict-related famine has been particularly severe since early 1988. The salient feature of both emergencies was the reticence and denial that characterized the response of the government in Khartoum and aggravated the emergencies. This attitude reflects two sets of factors that can be classified as regionalism and ethnicity. Each has political implications.

The regional factors include the country's size (the largest in Africa), its varied ecological and environmental conditions, its sparse population, and its rudimentary communication and transportation systems. All these factors are manifested in and compounded by disparities and inequities in the distribution system.

The ethnic factors include the racial, cultural, and religious diversity across the country. The most significant is the dichotomy between the Arab-Muslim North and the indigenously African South, which has a Christian elite. Diversity is by no means limited to that dualism, however. Differences within these categories are also profound and pronounced. These regional and ethnic diversities reflect vast distances from Khartoum in physical, political, and socioeconomic terms that explain the separation, if not alienation, of the national leadership from the rural populace.

These spatial and mental distances contributed to a vacuum of moral responsibility reflected in the government's persistent reluctance to provide relief to the affected population. The international media, initially stimulated by the dire conditions of the Ethiopian refugees fleeing into the Sudan, helped to alert the world in 1984 to the Sudan crisis. The international community then moved in to fill the moral vacuum and to pressure the government to be more responsive to the tragedy.

Once the government took the necessary steps, an unprecedented international relief operation was launched to compensate for the earlier neglect and to provide the government with the needed technical capacity to arrange for and distribute food. Many diverse donors, humanitarian organizations, and on-the-ground relief workers were involved in the emergency, with the United Nations and its specialized agencies coordinating the efforts. The experience of the emergency operations mounted in response to the drought-generated emergency laid the groundwork for the even more challenging international response to the conflict-related famine several years later.

The data and commentary that compose this volume have their origins in two recent studies of the emergency relief operations. The first was an evaluation conducted by one of the coauthors, Francis M. Deng, in 1986 at the request of the United Nations Office for

Emergency Operations in Africa (OEOA). The second was a case study of Operation Lifeline Sudan, conducted in 1990 by a team of independent researchers headed by the other coauthor, Larry Minear.

The first study, which took a detailed look at the UN-coordinated response to the drought emergency of 1983–86, sought to review the international community's experience while it was still fresh, distilling from it lessons that could strengthen the effectiveness of emergency relief activities in similar situations.

The OEOA was created on December 17, 1984, by the UN secretary-general in an effort to bring a higher level of political visibility and organizational coherence to UN relief efforts in Africa, which had hitherto taken a more country-by-country approach. The OEOA was set up, said one of its managers, "very much as the peacetime equivalent to putting the UN on a wartime footing."

The OEOA was based in New York with a liaison office in Geneva. It was directed by Bradford Morse, administrator of the UN Development Program, assisted by Maurice Strong as executive coordinator. Both men not only commanded great respect within the international system but also had far-reaching connections in the public and private sectors. Their remarkable contribution was perhaps most apparent in the fund-raising momentum generated by the OEOA within and outside the UN system.

The OEOA used such eminent organizations as the Inter-Action Council of the Former Heads of State and Government to mount a massive effort that climaxed in the March 1985 Geneva conference on the African emergency, at which the world demonstrated a generosity that surprised even the optimists. The generosity of the international community was commensurate with the magnitude of the disaster; the total amount mobilized for OEOA operations before the end of 1986 was $4.6 billion.

By the time the conference was convened, the OEOA estimated that some 30 million to 35 million people in twenty countries in sub-Saharan Africa faced starvation and death. When the OEOA closed on October 31, 1986, good rains had returned to most of the area, the food crisis had eased, and relief needs were abating. Serious emergencies continued only in Mozambique, Angola, Ethiopia, and the Sudan, where civil strife rather than the weather was the main culprit. During its two years of existence, in addition to helping raise the $4.6 billion in emergency assistance, the OEOA accelerated multilateral and bilateral relief operations in the region. The monitoring that had been performed by the OEOA was transferred to a newly created position, that of director of emergencies, reporting to the secretary-general.

To assess the OEOA's effectiveness in the Sudan, the evaluation during the latter part of 1986 sought out more than fifty persons who were or had been directly involved in the relief effort, both inside and outside the Sudan. Those interviewed included UN officials at headquarters and in the field, national and regional Sudanese government officials, leaders of the insurgent Sudan People's Liberation Movement, representatives of foreign governments and of nongovernmental organizations in the Sudan, university professors, journalists, and Sudanese at the local level. The names of those interviewed are listed in the appendix.

A companion study of OEOA effectiveness in neighboring Ethiopia was carried out at the same time by Ambassador Anders Forsse of Sweden. His study is referenced a number of times in this volume. The two evaluations were completed in late 1986.

During the evaluation of the response to the drought-generated famine in the North, conflict-related tragedy was simmering in the South but had not yet reached the boiling point. For that reason, the evolving civil war, which at the time had at most a limited effect on relief operations in the North, was only alluded to in the OEOA study.

Three years later, the magnitude of the conflict and its human consequences had reached unprecedented proportions. In March 1989 the international community launched another major relief initiative, Operation Lifeline Sudan. The initial Lifeline undertaking, which concentrated its efforts between April and September 1989, was the subject of the second study.

The review of Lifeline was carried out by an independent team of four African and three American researchers: Tabyiegen Agnes Abuom, Eshetu Chole, Koste Manibe, Abdul Mohammed, Jennefer Sebstad, Thomas G. Weiss, and Larry Minear. During the period from March 1990 through June 1990, the team interviewed about two hundred persons, some of them the same people who had been sought out for the earlier study. The focus of the initial evaluation had been on the response to the drought that in 1983–86 affected primarily large areas in the North. The later case study centered on the emergency in the South, which, while aggravated by drought, had its roots in the country's resurgent civil war. This volume recapitulates parts of the case study of Operation Lifeline Sudan that illuminate the problems of providing famine relief.[1]

This work thus places under a single cover the OEOA evaluation, which covers the years 1984–86, and the later case study of Operation Lifeline Sudan, which treats the years 1988–89. It also takes note of the roots of the drought-induced famine in 1983, the period between the major international relief initiatives, and the extension of Lifeline operations through 1990 and into 1991. It thus assesses famine and emergency relief operations in the years 1983–91.

The international emergency relief operations treated in this volume, and indeed their counterparts elsewhere in Africa and around the world, represent the best efforts of a wide circle of actors. Included, in addition to the people who needed such assistance themselves, are governmental organizations, nongovernmental groups, and individuals. The Sudan experience in 1984–86 and again in the heyday of Lifeline in 1989 was a triumph of humanitarian idealism and global solidarity that is rightly a cause for appreciation by the recipients and for satisfaction by those who provided such aid.

Acclaim notwithstanding, the analysis of the four challenges presented in this volume suggests that the experience was not without contradictions and ambivalences. Whatever the shortcomings of the relief operations, however, they developed during an emergency in which saving lives was the top priority. Any criticism, therefore, is intended not to question the need for emergency relief operations, but to improve such activities in the future. Past relief operations, critically and thoughtfully reviewed, may become the basis for more effective future activities. Indeed, the international public is coming to expect and to demand better performance.

Two methodological observations are in order. First, looking back at the crises, we often lack the original sense of urgency, sometimes bordering on panic, that characterized the desperate scramble to save lives. While nonoperational issues may loom larger in hindsight, this analysis does not intend to minimize the urgency that made it difficult to attend to broader issues at the time.

Second, much of the material in this volume is drawn from extensive interviews with major participants during the periods under review. Those interviews inform the conclusions reached and are frequently quoted in the text. Our general approach, particularly in the OEOA review, has been to reproduce such comments—many of which were shared in confidence—without attribution. Quotations and observations pertaining to Operation Lifeline Sudan are documented in the original study and referred to in the notes in this volume.

Finally, a word about the organization of the book itself. Chapter 1 presents the crises in the context of the salient facts about the country: its geography, its demography, and its regional politics, which affected the two emergency situations. It offers some observations on the underlying causes of famine, the attitudes of national governments, and evolving international perceptions.

Chapter 2, which treats drought-related famine during the mid-decade, and chapter 3, which examines conflict-related famine thereafter, discuss four problems exemplified in the responses to each crisis: the external nature of famine relief; the context in which relief is provided; the coordination of relief activities; and the ambivalence of the results of relief.

Looking to the future, chapter 4 suggests ways in which the international community, learning from the problems of relief operations in the Sudan, may strengthen such interventions in the future. The chapter also recognizes the increasingly positive international climate marking the end of the cold war, in particular the recent humanitarian intervention in Iraq, as an indicator of an emerging trend.

For a number of reasons, this review of emergency relief operations has a special timeliness. First, the emergency in the Sudan has continued apace during 1991–92, with an estimated 7 million to 9 million people still vulnerable to famine. Efforts by national authorities and the international community to assist them are lagging. In fact, in April 1992 the United Nations suspended relief operations altogether.

Second, recurrent food shortages in the Sudan and other sub-Saharan African countries have led to calls for recreating the OEOA or establishing some other structure in the United Nations with similar functions. A group of more than forty nongovernmental organizations wrote to UN Secretary-General Pérez de Cuéllar in June 1991, encouraging reestablishment of the OEOA. "We believe current famine conditions in the Horn of Africa and other African nations are potentially worse than those in 1984–86," they stated.

In response to the worsening crisis in the Sudan, Ethiopia, and Somalia, the secretary-general in July 1991 announced the strengthening of the unit for special emergency programs within the Department for Special Political Questions, Regional Co-operation, Decolonization and Trusteeship, to which the residual OEOA functions had been entrusted in late 1986. Once again, the world community recognized a need to move beyond ad hoc responses to crises in individual countries through an approach that would give higher visibility to the humanitarian crisis and greater coherence to international efforts.

Third, the United Nations is concerned with improving its response to emergencies. The Economic and Social Council discussed the problem in July 1991, the General Assembly discussed it in September and December 1991, and the issue is likely to engage the General Assembly in the years to come. Of special concern are refugees whose flight from persecution carries them across national borders and returnees and persons displaced within their own national borders who lack international protection and assistance.

The heads of state from seven major industrialized countries, meeting in mid-July 1991 in London, underlined the importance of these issues. "The recent tragedies in Bangladesh, Iraq and the Horn of Africa," observed the Economic Summit communiqué, "demonstrate the need to reinforce UN relief in coping with emergencies." The heads of state called for "moves to strengthen the coordination and to accelerate the effective delivery of all UN relief for major disasters." Boutros Boutros-Ghali, who became UN secretary-general on January 1, 1992, has a clear mandate to improve the structures for emergency humanitarian operations around the world. In early 1992 he appointed Swedish Ambassador Jan Eliasson to the new position of under-secretary-general for humanitarian affairs, following up on a resolution (46-182) approved by the General Assembly in December 1991.

Finally, there is much talk of a new international order in which the politicization that skewed the responses of governments and infiltrated the work of the United Nations during the cold war gives way to approaches that are less ideological and more directed toward need. By overriding Iraqi sovereignty to provide humanitarian assistance and protection to the Kurds, the UN Security Council has paved the way for the current discussion of a new humanitarian order in which governments are held—by force, if necessary—to higher standards of respect for human life.

Although the humanitarian content of an eventual new order has yet to be delineated, more effective responses to urgent crises such as those described in this volume will test the effectiveness of any new policies and institutional mechanisms. Much remains to be learned from recent emergency operations in the Sudan to guide the framing and implementation of a more effective international humanitarian response.

Chapter 1

Famine: Causes and Responses

During the past decade, international efforts to combat famine and food shortages around the globe have concentrated on the critical situations in sub-Saharan Africa. Throughout the 1980s across much of the African subcontinent, droughts, complicated by civil strife and debilitating economic problems, have caused widespread human suffering.

Famines in Africa and around the globe have frequently gone hand in hand with aberrations in weather. Drought has been famine's single most constant companion. Famines generally have multiple and mutually reinforcing causes, however, and immediate events such as meteorological fluctuations are only contributory factors. Some of these causes are problems in national agricultural policies and systems (inadequate or inappropriate incentives for producers, land tenure policies, or agricultural inputs such as credit, seeds, and fertilizers); malfunctioning of marketing, transportation, and other food distribution mechanisms; reduction of arable land through unsustainable agricultural practices; failure of production to keep pace with the increasing demands of a growing population; and inadequate resources to import additional foodstuffs. In the Sudan during the decade under review, these conditions, combined with drought and conflict and compounded by the indifference of political authorities, turned serious food shortages into outright famines.

Throughout these years, international attention directed toward the Sudan has been rivaled only by that accorded Ethiopia. The Sudan has seemed to offer, with tragic regularity, the proverbial worst case scenario. Widespread food needs have been denied, food has been used as a weapon, and outside assistance has been obstructed and frustrated. Problems and negative publicity notwithstanding, the country has received positive recognition for the relative successes of the UN Emergency Operation for the Sudan (UNEOS) in 1984–86, and Operation Lifeline Sudan in 1989.

The drought that triggered the famine in 1984 had been in the making for several years. As early as 1982, the people of Darfur and later the people in Kordofan and in the Red Sea Hills became concerned about the decrease in rainfall in their areas, predicting that severe famine might result. The crisis escalated in 1984 when the rains failed again, and the feared famine began in regions stretching across the country from west to east.

The United Nations mobilized a massive relief effort, which, during a two-year period beginning in late 1984, delivered about 1.5 million metric tons of food and provided the Sudan a variety of other assistance. The aid intervention involved an all-hands-on-deck approach by nongovernmental organizations (NGOs) and governments, with the UN system playing both coordinating and operational roles.

During the years of drought and famine in the northern Sudan, a civil war, which had been in remission from 1972 to 1983, was sputtering back to life in the southern Sudan. The conflict, which reflected an amalgam of economic, political, religious, and cultural differences between the largely Arab and Muslim North and the predominantly black South, where traditional religions and Christianity predominate, heated up markedly during 1986–88. In 1988 alone, an estimated 250,000 people, almost all of them civilians, lost their lives because of the conflict-related famine.

In early 1989 the international community responded to the grave humanitarian crisis by launching a second massive intervention, Operation Lifeline Sudan. Lifeline, involving governments and NGOs coordinated by the United Nations, mobilized some $200 million to $300 million in resources for the Sudan during 1989. It is widely credited with averting a repetition of the tragedy of 1988. Having won the consent of the two warring parties to the provision of international relief, Lifeline continued, though with less success, in 1990 and 1991 and into 1992.

During both famines, the crisis was aggravated by the reluctance of national political leaders to recognize the problem and to seek international relief aid, an attitude that contrasted sharply with international pressure for intervention. In each instance, the outcome involved a massive, if belated, international relief operation that helped offset the reticence, complacency, and technical incapacity of the government to provide relief.

THE GEOGRAPHIC CONTEXT

The Sudan is the largest country in Africa, nearly 1 million square miles, an area roughly equal to the size of Western Europe. Located at the meeting point of the Arab northern Africa and the sub-Saharan African countries, the Sudan borders eight countries: Libya and Egypt to the north; Ethiopia to the east; Kenya, Uganda, and Zaire to the south; and the Central African Republic and Chad to the west. Saudi Arabia, a ninth neighbor, lies across the Red Sea. The country stretches about 1,300 miles from the Sahara Desert in the north to the tropical rain forests in the south, and 1,000 miles from the Red Sea coast to the western border.

The land falls into four main zones of climate, vegetation, and topography: the dry, rocky desert and semidesert of the North; the undulating sand, passing from semidesert to savannah, lying south of the northern zone; a clay belt spreading eastward from southern Darfur to the rainlands and semidesert east of the Blue Nile and the main Nile, where annual rainfall increases to between eight and twenty-five inches; and the southern region, which ranges from rich savannah grassland to the thickly forested and humid jungle, rich with a variety of flora and fauna, with an annual rainfall ranging from about fifteen inches in the north to sixty inches on the Nile-Congo divide.[1]

The topography comprises mostly plains and hills forming a slope toward the Nile basin. The White and Blue Niles originate respectively from the Great Lakes of East Africa and the Ethiopian Highlands. The White Nile flows into the saucer-shaped swampy basin called the Sudd, an area of about 100,000 square kilometers, where half the water is wasted by evaporation and transpiration.[2] As the White Nile flows northward, the swamps turn into a region of thorny acacia forests and later into open, almost treeless plains. At Khartoum the White Nile is joined by the swifter, shorter Blue Nile.

The area lying between the Blue and the White Niles as they approach their confluence at Khartoum is called the Gezira, the Arabic word for island. The Gezira is a prime piece of arable land that has traditionally been the granary of the Sudan and is the site of vast irrigated cotton fields, backbone of the Sudanese economy since the colonial days.

These physical characteristics have a bearing on the emergency famine situation in the Sudan. They explain, for instance, why the

North more than the South is prone to drought-generated famine; on the whole the North is arid and dry, while the South is lush and wet. They also reflect not only a volatile variation of climatic and vegetational conditions in the two regions, but also an unusual vastness with contrastingly rudimentary means of transportation and poor communications.

Transportation was unquestionably the biggest single bottleneck during the emergency operations. The railroad system, a relic of the Anglo-Egyptian reconquest campaign, was first extended westward to El Obeid in Kordofan and later to Nyala in Darfur and Wau in the South. The soil under the rails is frequently washed away by the rains, incapacitating the railroad. The system has proved increasingly deficient over the years. The road system does not offer a better alternative. Apart from the Khartoum-Medani road, constructed in the late 1950s with funds from USAID, and the more recent Port Sudan–Khartoum road, many of the overland routes are beaten tracks in sandy or muddy soils, over which trucks snake their way with formidable difficulties.

THE DEMOGRAPHIC CONTEXT

The varied physical characteristics of the Sudan are matched by the ethnic composition of the country. Because of its size and location, the Sudan is an ethnic, linguistic, and religious microcosm of the African continent. The country is sparsely populated, with some 24 million people spread over nearly 1 million square miles. At least fifty major ethnic groupings compose the population; almost six hundred significant subgroups speak more than one hundred different languages. The 1956 national census, using oversimplified but pertinent criteria for ethnic, cultural, and tribal identification, grouped the population into Arabs (39 percent, all in the northern Sudan); Nilotics (9 percent, all in the South); Fur (in the West, 6 percent); Beja (in the East, 6 percent); Nubians (in the extreme North, 6 percent); and Nilo-Hamites (in the South, 5 percent). The same census found Arabic spoken by 51 percent of the Sudanese population, Nilotic languages by 18 percent, and non-Arabic northern and central Sudanese languages by 12 percent. The census found the population to be 70 percent Muslim and 4 percent Christian, with the rest adhering to traditional religious beliefs.

The ethnic composition of the Sudan reflects a complex process of Arabization and Islamization, which affected parts of the North in varying degrees but did not extend to the South in any significant degree. The integration between the immigrant Arabs and the indigenous population of the North goes as far back as recorded history. Egyptian and Nubian rulers periodically invaded each other's territory. Authority shifted back and forth, a process that resulted in ethnic and cultural interaction and assimilation. Through Egypt and directly across the Red Sea, Arab men without their women penetrated the lands of the Nubians to the north and the Beja to the east, trading and settling among the indigenous populations, intermarrying with them, and becoming assimilated into Sudanese society and culture.

Before the advent of Islam, most of the northern part of the country was under the rule of three Christian kingdoms along the Nile valley. These rulers converted large sections of the northern Sudanese population. They prospered until they were gradually undermined by Islam in the seventh century and were overthrown in the sixteenth century.

The Arab-Islamic empire invaded Nubian and Beja territories with a superior military technology that gave them an advantage in the eventual peace treaties. The treaties enhanced the economic, social, cultural, and religious status of the Arab Muslims by giving them free access into the Sudan, allowing them to move and settle as they wished, and safeguarding their commercial interests, religious freedom, and personal safety. Their privileged status, contrasting sharply with that of the Negro, a heathen and a potential slave, made the Arab Muslims even more envied than they had been during the pre-Islamic period. Through the system of matrilineal succession prevalent in that part of the country, the descendants of these Arabs inherited positions of leadership but identified with their fathers according to the Arab patriarchal system, eventually turning the society into the patrilineal model that began to perpetuate the Arab-Islamic identity.

Arabization and Islamization gradually spread throughout the North. They did not supplant or eradicate the existing tribal order or indigenous religious beliefs and practices but instead built on these indigenous factors in a way that facilitated the acceptance of Arabism and Islam. The process did not affect all the peoples of the northern Sudan to the same degree. Throughout the North, those who claim to be Arabs and trace their genealogies to Arabia—in the case of the more important lineages to the tribe and to the family of the prophet Muhammad—are in fact of mixed Arab and African blood.

These ethnic diversities within the North affect the identification of the various northern groups among one another and between the center and the periphery. They help explain the distance—physical, social, and psychological—during the drought emergency between the rulers in Khartoum and the affected populations of the West and the East.

The processes of Arabization and Islamization did not affect the southern part of the country, partly because of the hostile natural environment, which acted as a barrier to Arab penetration, and partly because of the resistance of the warrior Nilotic tribes, the Dinka, the Nuer, and the Shilluk, among others. This has left the country with a legacy of racial, ethnic, cultural, and religious diversity and disparity that continues to be a characteristic feature.

The complex configuration of the country is thus reduced to a North-South dualism, which reflects the perception, if not the reality, of racial, ethnic, cultural, and religious differences, with corresponding political and economic disparities. The North, which constitutes two-thirds of the land and population, has been politically, economically, and culturally dominant and more developed, with notable internal disparities between the central region and the peripheral regions in the West and the East. The subordinate South, which constitutes the remaining third of both land and population, has remained largely undeveloped.

One ethnic group of the South, the Ngok Dinka, occupies the territory at the southernmost point of Kordofan in the North, with its administrative headquarters at Abyei. Even long before the advent of colonial rule, the leaders of this group maintained relatively cordial relations with the leaders of the Missirya Arab tribes to the north. Through those diplomatic relations, they were able to mitigate the slave raids from Arab tribes against their people and fellow Dinka farther south. With the advent of condominium, Ngok leaders chose to be affiliated administratively with Kordofan to maintain their relations with their northern neighbors and to ensure the protection of their people by the provincial and central government authorities.

As southerners living in the North, the Ngok Dinka have played a bridging role in the North-South context similar to the role postulated for the Sudan between North and sub-Saharan Africa. Paradoxically, however, Abyei became one of the areas where starvation was worst. People, especially children, died in masses within easy reach of government and international relief services simply because the government identified them as southerners and therefore part of the enemy camp. Even those who moved from Abyei to northern areas such as Muglad, Babanusa, and El Dhein, where food was plentiful, were allowed to starve to death because they were Dinkas and therefore southerners and enemies.

The disparities and mutual animosities between the North and the South were reinforced through most of the nineteenth century, beginning with the Turko-Egyptian rule of the Ottoman Empire in 1821, continuing with the Mahdist revolution that overthrew it in 1885, and extending to the Anglo-Egyptian condominium of 1898, which was, in effect, British rule. After initial military repression and suppression of resistance, the British eventually established peace and stability under the rule of law. But they also reinforced the gulf between the North and the South through their infamous separatist Southern Policy, which kept Arab-Islamic influence out of the South and preserved the people in their indigenous state, without any development, except for the modest "civilizing" influence of the Christian missions.

THE POLITICAL CONTEXT

Since famine is ultimately the result of poverty and the denial of entitlement to food, these regional and ethnic animosities contributed to the fact that the most conspicuous victims of the two emergency situations were from the West, the East, and the South. The politics of regionalism and ethnicity manifests itself in the vacuum of moral responsibility implicit in the negative responses of the central government to both famines and the need for international intervention.

Regional and ethnic cleavages contributed to the southern perception that independence, which was largely the result of nationalism in the North supported by Egypt, was merely a change of masters. Southern fear of Arab domination triggered the August 1955 mutiny by a southern battalion that ignited a region-wide rebellion. The mutineers were later persuaded by the outgoing British governor-general to surrender. Northern political parties then promised to give the South's call for a federal relationship with the North serious consideration, providing the basis for the unanimous declaration of independence on January 1, 1956.

The South's demand for federalism was subsequently rejected, and postcolonial governments sought to unify the country through a centralized system and assimilationist policies of Arabization and Islamization. The response developed into a separatist armed struggle led by the Southern Sudan Liberation Movement, whose military wing, the Anya-Nya, took its name from a deadly insect in the region. The fighting dragged on for seventeen years. In 1972 the movement and the military government of Jaafar Mohamed Nimeiri agreed on a compromise embodied in the Addis Ababa Agreement, which granted the South regional autonomy.

The agreement was acclaimed throughout Africa and the world as a victory for unity in diversity from which many developing countries could learn. The international community responded generously to the relief, rehabilitation, and resettlement of the returning refugees and the displaced people in the South. The United States was among the most generous in its response. The Sudan, along with other Arab countries, had severed diplomatic ties with the United States after the Arab-Israeli Six-Day War in 1967. Now, however, the Sudan reestablished bilateral relations, the first Arab country to do so. Nimeiri soon won a reputation as a peacemaker with a moderating influence in the region.

With peace and stability achieved, Sudanese diplomacy was effectively mobilized to promote international cooperation in the development of the country. This coincided with the oil boom of the early 1970s, which released large amounts of petrodollars into circulation. The Sudan became an example of trilateral cooperation between Arab capital and Western technology for the development of the vast potential in agricultural wealth.

A number of Arab funds became actively involved in the Sudan's ambitious programs of agricultural development. The Arab Authority for Agricultural Development was created with headquarters in Khartoum and designated the Sudan as the first country in which to concentrate its activities. One irony of the situation was that the Sudan soon turned from being a promising breadbasket to being an embarrassing basket case, an extraordinary turn of events for the otherwise seemingly successful President Nimeiri. This development helps explain not only the famine but also Nimeiri's response to it.

Domestic developments, both positive and negative, closely paralleled Nimeiri's regional and international diplomacy. Nimeiri's profile in the West was greatly enhanced by his mutual hostilities with both Muammar Qadhafi of Libya and the Marxist Mengistu Haile Mariam of Ethiopia. His image as a moderate and a peacemaker, which contrasted with that of these two neighbors, was also enhanced by his support of the Camp David accords between Egypt and Israel. Nimeiri's support of the Camp David agreement in part followed from his conciliatory domestic policy toward the South, which in turn reinforced his friendship with the United States.

Contradictory trends were beginning to emerge, however, in Nimeiri's domestic policies. The fundamentalists and the sectarian political parties continued to oppose the government, organizing military resistance from bases in Libya and Ethiopia. In 1976 they infiltrated the country with supporters and foreign mercenaries trained and armed by Libya and staged a ferocious attack. They failed to overthrow the regime but left Nimeiri severely shaken, especially as Sadiq al-Mahdi, the leader of the opposition, openly admitted responsibility and vowed to try again.

Although Sadiq al-Mahdi was tried in a court of law and condemned to death in absentia, he moved freely in Arab and European capitals, where Nimeiri's extradition requests went unheeded. Only a year later, Nimeiri met secretly with Sadiq al-Mahdi and agreed on a national reconciliation that resulted in appointment to the government of opposition members, including Hassan al-Turabi, the leader of the Muslim Brotherhood.

Soon Nimeiri's differences with the opposition, especially with Sadiq al-Mahdi, began to reemerge. Perhaps to undercut the religious authority of the fundamentalists and the sectarian leaders, Nimeiri adopted a religious agenda aimed at Islamizing the state. The Muslim Brotherhood shrewdly decided to cooperate with him in an uneasy alliance, fraught with mutual mistrust. Together they worked on revising the laws of the country to conform to Islamic standards.

In September 1983, Nimeiri imposed *shari'a* (Islamic law) through laws that became known as the September Laws, to distinguish them from proper *shari'a* and therefore render them a legitimate target of attack by opposition Muslim leaders who were themselves committed to the implementation of *shari'a*. Religious leaders other than the Muslim Brotherhood opposed the laws as an exploitation and perversion of Islam. Ustadh Mahmoud Mohamed Taha, the founding leader of the Republican Brotherhood, a liberal school of Islamic thought, was tried and executed for apostasy because of his opposition to the September laws. This further alienated support for the regime both at home and abroad.

Nimeiri's stronghold in the South was also beginning to crack, mostly because of his own shifts in policy. Because of the compromises he had been forced to make with his opposition in the North, he gradually began to undermine the agreement he had reached with the South in 1972.

Nimeiri decreed the division of the South into three regions. The government began to transfer the absorbed Anya-Nya forces to the North, allegedly to foster integration, but actually to reduce the South's ability to resist. One unit at the Bor garrison resisted, triggering the resumption of hostilities in 1983 and the creation of the Sudan People's Liberation Movement (SPLM) and its military arm, the Sudan People's Liberation Army (SPLA). Both were led by Colonel John Garang de Mabior, a Sudanese Army officer with a Ph.D. in agricultural economics from Iowa State University.

The economy had also taken a turn for the worse. The Sudan's image as a suitable place for investing petrodollars had stimulated a development strategy with unmonitored and unscrutinized borrowing for projects that were not productive. With earnings from cotton down and the bills for imported oil soaring, the country could not meet even its basic needs. Debts began to mature, and the pressures for debt servicing mounted beyond the Sudan's capacity to pay. Pressures for structural adjustment from the International Monetary Fund forced the government to cut subsidies for essential commodities and to adopt other austerity measures that inflicted much hardship on the people.

The more the regime felt threatened by political and economic pressures, the more repressive it became and the more it relied on foreign support for its security. So alienated from the domestic constituencies did Nimeiri become that even the Muslim Brotherhood, an ally in the promotion of Islam, fell from favor, accused of having exploited the Islamic banking system to enrich itself and to undermine the economy. Ironically, the rising influence of the National Islamic Front, the post-Nimeiri political reincarnation of the Muslim Brotherhood, is attributed to its financial and economic gains under Nimeiri.

These developments were critical to Nimeiri's insecurity as he pondered whether to admit the famine emergency, invite massive foreign involvement, and risk exposing the regime's fundamental failure, or try to contain the crisis through denial in the hope that it might prove to be less devastating than the reports predicted. Nevertheless, the famine contributed to Nimeiri's overthrow by popular uprising in April 1985.

After a transitional government coaxed the country back to parliamentary democracy within a year, Sadiq al-Mahdi was prime minister in a series of coalition governments characterized by weakness, uncertainty, and instability. The conflict in the South continued unabated. Conflict-related famine reached its peak. Three years later military rule returned, on June 30, 1989, when a group of previously unknown middle-rank officers seized power in the name of a "Revolution for National Salvation," supported, if not masterminded, by the National Islamic Front.

This event increased the distance between Khartoum and the peripheral or disadvantaged regions, especially because the rural areas of the West and the East were strongholds of the sectarian political parties targeted by the self-proclaimed revolution for national salvation. Political factors thus contributed to the complacency regarding famine. The regime had declared as its motto, "We produce what we eat and eat what we produce." The famine emergency thus caused great moral and political embarrassment, the more so because the origin of the expected relief was the Christian West.

The South has resisted Arab domination and marginalization through armed struggle partly because it is the region that is the most disadvantaged. According to Tigani al-Tayeb, a Sudanese politician, while people in other regions of the country had options for political participation, southerners had few opportunities for effective action.[3]

Khartoum is remote not only from the marginalized population of the South, West, and East, but also from the rural tribal masses as a whole. While sectarian political leadership derives its support from less sophisticated followers in the rural areas, it grants them little leverage in exchange for their support. The disparity between the urban and the rural areas has long been recognized, even though the country was administered through the tribal system during the period of colonial rule and for much of the period of independence. Ibrahim Bedri predicted at the dawn of independence a reaction to the injustices against the tribes:

> When these tribesmen attain sufficient political consciousness, their tribal bond will make their complete transfer to the higher strata of the "nation" easier than the transfer of the atomistic agglomeration of the townsfolk. This peculiarity of the tribal system should not be overlooked. . . . A day may come when the tribal system gives way to a better system but until such times come there is no practical way of hurrying up this process, nor have we any right before such time comes to deny tribal leaders and chiefs their rights. If we alienate them, we will be sowing the seeds of hatred and suspicion between them and the townsfolk without achieving much.[4]

These prophetic words have become reality, especially following the abolition of chieftainship in the northern Sudan and its weakening in the South during the early years of the Nimeiri regime. The capacity of the traditional leaders to maintain order and a sustainable pattern of life has diminished ever since, and no adequate modern alternatives have been devised. Some logistical problems of delivery and distribution during the drought-induced famine can be attributed to the collapse of the tribal administrative system, which the Nimeiri regime eventually regretted.

The emergency situation emanating from the two famines, the inability of the government to respond, and the difficulties in delivering food to the needy reflect the breakdown of the system and highlight the fundamental problem of regional and ethnic cleavages reflected in the urban-rural, North-South dichotomies. It took outsiders—the international relief community—to construct a bridge across the divides.

POVERTY AND UNDERDEVELOPMENT

Poverty and underdevelopment as endemic causes for the recurrent famines in Sudanese history were reviewed at a June 1991 conference on the Sudan in Washington, D.C., cosponsored by the Sudan government and the Middle East Institute. The Sudan's ambassador to the United States, Abdalla A. Abdalla, himself a professor of agriculture and a former minister of agriculture, asked why countries like the Sudan and others in sub-Saharan Africa suffer from recurrent famines. He began with the legacies of colonialism. While it brought together many tribal or ethnic groups into the unitary framework of the nation-state, colonialism, he observed, also partitioned sub-Saharan Africa into fifty-plus countries and then extracted many of the continent's natural resources from them. Colonial policies oriented agriculture toward exports. The Sudanese production of cotton for British manufacturers is a prime example. Production, research, and extension services related to food crops for local consumption languished in comparison with cash crops directed to the needs of the colonial powers.

The colonial scramble for Africa created ethnic and territorial tensions and conflicts that destabilized the continent, aggravating the structural constraints to development. Following independence, tensions were in turn heightened by the cold war, which, Abdalla pointed out, "caused considerable damage to economic development through feeding internal political and ideological conflicts." Political instability resulting from colonial fragmentation has played itself out in more than sixty successful coup d'états in thirty-five years and in eleven civil wars still raging on the continent in the 1990s. Factors beyond the control of developing countries themselves thus combine to exacerbate underdevelopment and susceptibility to famine. This has been particularly true in the Sudan.

As Professor Abdalla noted, "Food and poverty problems are also a product of mismanagement, lack of improved technologies for increased productivity, misguided policies, strategies and priority-setting over the past two decades." Favoritism of more privileged urban interests at the expense of the poorer rural masses is a matter of record. Well endowed with the natural and human ingredients of agricultural productivity, the Sudan after thirty-six years of independence is still "failing to provide food security for its people."[5]

A combination of historical factors, government policies, and international developments made the 1980s particularly vexing for the Sudan. During the 1970s, the Sudan, with the encouragement of investments from the industrialized West and oil-producing Arab countries, had envisioned itself as the breadbasket of North Africa and the Middle East. That optimistic outlook gave way in the 1980s to the grim realities of stagnation in the country's agricultural and other sectors.

Although food production during the decade generally held its own against rapid population growth of 3.1 percent, per capita income declined an average of 4.7 percent a year between 1980 and 1987, and inflation averaged some 30 percent a year. Despite some good crop years, especially during the early part of the decade, problems of transportation and distribution hindered the availability of food. In fact, one of the major uses of emergency relief funds in 1984–86 was to transport existing supplies of food from one region within the Sudan to another.

By mid-decade, the Sudan's economy had become a matter of international concern. Earnings on cotton and other major commodity exports were down, while import bills and government spending were soaring. In 1985 the government, at the urging of the International Monetary Fund, ended subsidies on basic foods and gasoline. Strikes and riots ensued. During the decade as a whole, the nation's debt grew fourfold, to more than $12 billion. Once again, the Sudan's situation was not unlike that of other sub-Saharan countries, for whom these years have been described as "Africa's lost decade of development."[6]

Civil war became an obstacle to the nation's economic health and progress. The war also destroyed the resource base of the rural southern population, especially in the areas bordering the North. Entire villages were rendered uninhabitable. Some of the displaced sought refuge elsewhere within the rural North or in cities. Wherever the displaced took refuge, they were far less able to provide for their own food needs. Traditional food production and distribution, including survival techniques during famine, were not only disrupted as a by-product of the war. Their disruption was also a strategic goal of the warring parties.[7]

By the end of the decade, according to the government, the war was costing more than $1 million a day. Defense expenditures doubled in the short period between 1984–85 and 1987–88 as the fighting escalated. Late in the decade, after good rains had returned to sub-Saharan Africa, serious food shortages continued only in countries beset by civil war—Angola, Ethiopia, Liberia, Mozambique, Somalia, and the Sudan—underscoring the link between conflict and famine.

In the Sudan, as tribal militias burgeoned and civil order broke down, violence became widespread and environmental and economic conditions deteriorated. Responding to the pressures from encroaching desertification, drought, and famine, Arab tribes moved southward with their herds into land traditionally inhabited by the Dinka. Clashes over pastures and sources of water supply soon took on ethnic overtones, which fed into the North-South conflict. The government capitalized on these tensions, using tribal militias to fight the SPLA. The confrontation also had crude religious undercurrents, with the Dinka seen as heathens and thus legitimate targets of Islamic *jihad*. With the total devastation of Dinka land and its resource base, the mutual reinforcement of the vicious circle linking the environment, drought, conflict, and famine was complete.

In summary, while drought and subsequent crop failure triggered the 1983–86 famine in the North and the later famine in the South, the Sudan's existing underdevelopment, the government's policies, and the incapacity of the country to provide for the affected population were in reality their major causes. The situation dramatizes the lethal interaction of poverty, policy, environment, conflict, and famine. The Sudan was like a weakened body whose lowered resistance to disease made it more susceptible to illness. Once afflicted by disease, the body was powerless to mobilize its natural coping mechanisms. A healthier body with the capacity and resources to resist infection would have been more resilient.

OFFICIAL ATTITUDES

Of almost equal importance in the etiology of famine are the attitudes of the political authorities. Given the slowness with which famines evolve, the passivity of officialdom can accelerate the development of serious food shortages into full-blown famines. Conversely, assertive action can avoid widespread starvation.

Famines in the Sudan and other sub-Saharan African countries have come and gone, most of them falling within the impressive abilities of rural populations to cope. The Sudanese themselves have named famines according to their origins, whether in natural causes such as drought, locusts, or cattle disease or in events of human making such as war or forced migrations.

In a recent study of the 1984–86 famine in Darfur, Alex de Waal categorized the Sudan's famines according to the hardship they inflicted. The first category refers to shortage of grain or availability of food only at prices people could not afford. The result was that people experienced *hunger*. Famines of this sort occurred in 1926–27, 1930, 1937, 1939, 1941–42, 1949–50, 1969, and 1973. People responded by tightening their belts and by doing their best to stretch scarce resources, relying on kinship, on more fortunate neighboring communities, and on supplementary food sources. Intercommunal marriages and commodity exchanges were among the structural means of ensuring against famine.

A second set of famines bore the names of various wild foods sought out during periods of more serious hardship. During normal times collecting such foods was socially stigmatized. In such circumstances famine meant not only hunger but also *destitution*, as in the Darfur famine of 1950.

A third kind of famine was characterized by hardship more serious still. Such famines were given names "powerfully symbolic of the breakdown of society, of being outcast, solitary, or dependent: all opposites to the ideals of belonging, community, and autonomy."[8] The result of famines of this severity was *death*, reflecting the failure of the coping mechanisms that saw people through most hard times.

In most famines, particularly in earlier years, people were more isolated from the central government and had to depend on cooperation with their neighbors or other local measures. Under those circumstances, attitudes of the authorities did not have a major bearing on people's survival. A comparison of two historic famines, in 1888–92 and in 1912–14, illustrates the growing dependence of people on the central government and the effect of negative and positive responses by the authorities.

During the reign of Khalifa Abdullahi, a famine of catastrophic proportions occurred, caused by both drought and the devastations of the intertribal upheavals of the Mahdist state. Abdullahi had succeeded the Mahdi, who died shortly after his hard-won victory against the Turko-Egyptian administration in the Sudan. The Mahdist regime hardly established a credible system of control over the country or provided protection against a famine of such unprecedented magnitude.

The killing famine of 1912–14, also caused by a combination of natural factors and civil strife, resulted in massive population displacement and many deaths. But the condominium administration, unlike the theocracy of Khalifa Abdullahi, was a modern government. Though alien, it exercised effective control over significant portions of the country and felt a sense of responsibility for the people's welfare. What distinguished that famine from its predecessor, therefore, was the more positive role of government authorities in providing relief. In the earlier period, the government had disregarded the welfare of citizens except that of a select group of fellow tribesmen, officials, soldiers, and their families. In the later period, the more activist approach of the government spared people the indignities of their earlier struggle for survival.

While the historical record indicates an increasing sense of responsibility over time by central governments in Khartoum, causes of food shortages are too diverse and the responses of the authorities too varied to support any facile generalization about nineteenth-century negligence and twentieth-century responsibility. In fact, official responses to both the drought-induced famine of 1983–86 and the conflict-related famine of 1987–91 had elements of each approach. In both instances, the economic conditions of the country played a role in the deterioration of serious food shortages into widespread famines and in the difficulties encountered by relief efforts. Poor infrastructure and, in particular, poor facilities for transportation, in themselves features of underdevelopment, seriously impeded the delivery and distribution of relief supplies.

The two periods are distinguished from each other not by underdevelopment and the general incapacity of the government to provide relief, but by official attitudes. While indifference abounded during the regime of President Nimeiri, there was little official animosity toward rural populations of the North. The government's anxiety lest widespread food shortages might expose its weakness or threaten its future did not translate into hostility toward those who were suffering. It reflected indifference bordering on irresponsibility.

During this period, the government on occasion rounded up people who had sought refuge in Khartoum, southerners escaping the civil war and westerners seeking food security, and relocated them either back to their places of origin or in an outlying district of the central region. This police action, which became known as *kesha*, was perceived by the non-Arab southerners and westerners as racially motivated. It aroused a great deal of resentment not only among the people but also among the political leaders of the South and the West.

In the later period the North-South conflict made southern Sudanese objects of active hatred by a significant number of the leading personalities in the government. Widespread starvation among the southern Sudanese dramatized a profound political contradiction: despite assertions to the contrary, the government did not identify itself with the South and failed to provide for the people over whom it claimed sovereignty. Although the government used the massive influx of southerners into the North for propaganda purposes, claiming that it indicated the unpopularity of the SPLM-SPLA and greater trust in the North and the government, it also feared the southern population in and around Khartoum as a fifth column for the rebel movement. Later the government was torn between encouraging the return of southerners to their areas of origin in the war zone and fearing that, once there, they would then support the SPLM-SPLA. That ambivalence still characterizes the attitude of the government toward southerners living in the North.

For its part, the leadership of the insurgent SPLA did not treat seriously enough the suffering of civilians in the southern towns under government control. The SPLA took the attitude that southerners who chose to remain under the control of the government did so at their own risk, if not in actual betrayal of the cause. They were, in other words, collaborating with the enemy and should face the consequences. Such attitudes on each side vastly complicated the task of the international relief organizations.

The famine predicted in the North for 1991 and the attitude of the Islamic revolutionary government in Khartoum indicated that political authorities were accepting greater responsibility but that ideological or pragmatic political considerations were hindering action. Once again, the dispossessed masses seemed likely to fall victim to morally insensitive political calculations. And once again, the international community was stepping in to fill the moral vacuum.

Beginning in August and September 1990, international observers foresaw a famine of "biblical proportions" and actively pressed the Sudanese government to appeal for outside aid. Khartoum officials, speaking more cautiously of a "food gap," deferred action until more detailed assessments based on expected harvests could be made. The government's inaction led to sharp criticism by the media and by aid agencies, which perceived the government's position as a delaying tactic.

Three separate international teams reviewed the situation during the final months of 1990. The government, deferring action until the reports were completed, requested only a modest 35,000 tons in international food aid. During December the UN Food and Agriculture Organization confirmed sizable crop shortfalls, and the World Food Program estimated that throughout the country some 7.7 million people were at nutritional risk. Filling the need would require a staggering 1.145 million metric tons of food aid.

The continuing debate about the food crisis was the subject of a BBC documentary broadcast in April 1991. The program recalled that in September 1990 the governor of Darfur had sounded the alarm, confirming warnings already issued by private relief organizations. Evidence of massive food shortages was beyond dispute, but another six months elapsed before a major international response was mobilized. The documentary distributed the blame for the delay and the resulting famine deaths among the Sudan's harsh government, which was reluctant to admit the failure of its policies and to acknowledge the needs of its people; unyielding donors, who insisted on forcing Khartoum to say "famine" before they would provide help; and a passive United Nations, which was unwilling to confront the Sudanese and other governments with humanitarian imperatives. "The politics of food," concluded the program, "have taken precedence over the hunger of a nation."

In late 1991 a leading member of the National Islamic Front emphatically denied any threat of famine in the Sudan. He asserted that the country had ample supplies of food, that people were well fed, and that the cries of famine came only from foreign agencies seeking to finance their operations and to ensure jobs for their staffs. He implied that relief operations had become a self-sustaining industry in need of a cause. Does such an attitude reflect a gross miscalculation by the alarmed international community or a total lack of moral concern and responsibility by Sudanese leaders? Might there be some truth in what appears to be a cynical, if not sinister, attitude of the rulers? These questions, to be pursued later, certainly indicate a tension between old, parochial, largely indifferent government attitudes and an emerging expectation that governments will provide famine relief for the masses in cooperation with the international community.

It should be acknowledged that the massive starvation that was predicted by foreign observers as virtually inevitable even with international assistance did not in fact occur. Quite the contrary, by mid-1992 the government was able to announce a significant food surplus and anticipated beginning to export food by 1993. Although the ongoing dependency of the war-stricken South on food aid remained a tragic irony, this discrepancy between predictions by the international community and the realities on the ground raises serious questions of credibility, particularly regarding the allegation that relief operations have become a self-perpetuating industry. Nevertheless, it is essential that this credibility gap not be allowed to nourish complacency on the part of the international community, which, if anything, should risk erring on behalf of providing for the needy and the dispossessed.

What light do recent experiences throw on government attitudes as a major cause of famine? On the negative side, deferring action costs precious time needed to organize and to mount relief operations. Many lives are lost in the process. Yet the Sudanese government, even as it delayed in responding to the worsening food crisis while awaiting a more accurate assessment of needs, implicitly recognized that sovereign governments are expected to respond to the needs of hungry people. In eventually requesting aid, the government acknowledged that the primary responsibility for providing relief assistance rests with the authorities themselves and that the international community has an obligation to assist.

The circumscribed obligation to human suffering shown by the Mahdists in the last century is giving way to a more generally acknowledged acceptance of responsibility to avoid famine. That sense of responsibility is now shared by Sudanese political authorities and the wider international community. This is true even though it is sometimes honored only in the breach.

EMERGING GLOBAL PERSPECTIVES

An international code of conduct with universally accepted standards for governments and external actors is clearly evolving, even though its observance is still constrained by regional, ethnic, and religious differences. Because the failures of internal processes have such tragic consequences for those who fall victim to famine, increased international attention, monitoring, and timely action are needed.

The international community now has means for overcoming the indifference of governments that were not available at the time of the nineteenth-century famines or even earlier in the twentieth century. Resources that may be deployed in a needy country are more available internationally now than they were in the previous century. They can be used to fill a moral vacuum, to overcome problems within a country that contribute to hunger, and to offset the incapacity of governments to provide relief for their needy populations. As a result, political authorities today find it increasingly difficult to treat the right to food as negotiable and to brutalize civilian populations with impunity.

The role of the media and of aroused international public opinion in publicizing needs and holding governments accountable for their acknowledged responsibility to act has now been well documented. Both relief interventions reviewed in this volume benefited from the mobilization of such concern. Particularly in the case of Operation Lifeline Sudan, the glare of international publicity was instrumental in holding the protagonists to their moral commitments.

To the extent that governments can be held to commitments made in the UN Charter, the Geneva Conventions and Protocols, and various human rights covenants, the disappearance of famine will be hastened. "The major obstacle to eliminating famine," concluded an international consultation, "remains the destruction or interdiction of civilian food supplies in zones of armed conflict."[9] This assertion reflects the view that improved early warning systems and other technological advances have virtually eliminated forces of nature as a cause of famine. Famine today is a function of the conscious strategies of governments and opposition groups.

The fact that famine is a recurrent feature in the Sudan and elsewhere in sub-Saharan Africa suggests that relief should be designed not only to keep people alive until a particular food deficit is past but to decrease their vulnerability to future food shortages. Since famine has its roots in poverty and powerlessness, emergency operations are needed to undergird the resilience of the affected populations. Nongovernmental organizations have become an increasingly respectable alternative to direct government-to-government assistance. Humanitarian assistance, through people-to-people channels, can help to bridge the North-South gap. This alternative channel is coming into its own with the end of the cold war and the consequent removal of strategic incentives to international assistance.

Relief operations that are pursued without using local resources, enlisting local populations, or building local institutions may not enable people to regain control of their own future. At the same time, relief may itself be an investment in a relief-free future. Relief and development needs and opportunities are thus closely interrelated. Because droughts and famines have been an integral part of the Sudan's history, durable solutions must be found.

Professor Abdalla is surely right in concluding that in the Sudan, as throughout the region, "what is required is a massive collective effort to enable sub-Saharan African countries to achieve food self-reliance, food security and economic growth. That will require political stability which in turn is dependent on the resolution of internal conflicts, and prevalence of effective governance based on peoples' free participation and transparency in making government policies."[10]

With the end of the cold war, sub-Saharan Africa is no longer a region of active ideological jousting between the superpowers. Relief remains the only viable option for the West, involving both those who produce food in excess and those driven by humanitarian concerns. This source of support can be subversive not only of the economies of the recipient countries, but also of people's sense of dignity and independence. The same support, however, can also be used creatively to foster self-sustaining development from within. Poverty, environmental degradation, and chronic conflict will continue to generate famine or gaps in food sufficiency and therefore the need for relief. The challenge is whether this tragedy, combined with the motivation of the West to assist, can be turned into self-sustaining development and international cooperation.

Governments committed to famine relief might also be expected to support medium-term reconstruction and longer-term development. Cutbacks in international development assistance to the Sudan during the 1980s, however, reflected not only a lack of strategic incentives for development assistance but also the unhappiness of potential donors with the policies of the host government. The reductions in aid probably increased the country's vulnerability to food shortages.

An understanding of the causes of famine should inform international efforts to mount effective emergency relief operations and link them with rehabilitation and self-sustaining development. A historical perspective underscores the view that food shortages, however recurrent, can be addressed in such a way as to preempt their deterioration into famine. International attention increasingly focuses on indifferent political authorities and on specific safeguards and sanctions that make them accountable for their actions. The international community now has a chance, through improved cooperation, to eradicate famine.

THE CHALLENGES

This volume focuses on the challenges that confront relief operations. The problems that are inherent in humanitarian interventions cannot be avoided; they can only be managed, whether creatively or poorly. Understanding the problems enhances the chances for achieving the necessary balance in formulating and implementing programs. None of the available alternatives is completely satisfactory.

As mentioned in the introduction, the challenges cluster in four areas: the external nature of humanitarian interventions; the relationship between relief activities and endemic problems; the coordination of relief initiatives; and the ambivalent results of relief operations. Each of these challenges is present when the international community responds to a natural disaster such as the Sudan's drought-induced famine of 1983–86. Each problem takes on additional complexity when an emergency involves famine that is rooted in conflict, as in the Sudan crisis of 1987–91.

International relief operations are undertaken when national leadership and capability have proved unequal to the task of meeting the needs of the population. The first challenge thus concerns the external nature of such relief, which represents at the same time its greatest strength and its most serious weakness.

Enormous resources from around the world were placed at the disposal of relief agencies in the Sudan. The Sudan received external assistance in excess of $1 billion in 1984–86. This aid is widely credited with averting massive starvation, although the number of lives saved is impossible to quantify and many lives were lost despite energetic efforts to save them.

Similarly, Operation Lifeline Sudan mobilized an estimated $200 million to $300 million in 1989. These resources injected an international dimension into what would otherwise have remained domestic issues. However, the value of food aid was probably less important than the benefit of breaking food prices maintained by local merchants at high levels. The presence of international aid personnel in 1989 also helped restrain abuse of civilians and moderated the conduct of the war by both the government and the armed opposition, the Sudan People's Liberation Army.

On the negative side, the scale of the operations made the Sudanese feel overwhelmed by and excluded from the relief effort. They had no sense of being partners in the effort. The emphasis on external assistance further blurred the need for local people and institutions to view their own efforts as ultimately critical to their survival.

Reflecting on extensive field work in Darfur in 1984–85, one observer concluded that "all too often famines are discussed as though the successes and failures of relief were the most important factor in survival." In reality, however, "food aid was not the most important element in surviving the famine. This does not mean that the aid programmes were not important, just that they were less important than the people who worked on them and publicized them often believed."[11] The OEOA study noted the remarkable resourcefulness and resilience of the imperiled people themselves, who used survival techniques that were successful even though they did not measure up to global standards of human dignity.

The national humiliation Sudanese authorities associated with OEOA operations in 1984–86 kept them from more active cooperation with international agencies later in the decade. The backlash may have contributed to the government's unwillingness to acknowledge the scale of the need in 1988. The Muslim fundamentalist government resisted acknowledging food shortages in 1990–91 partly because it feared that the Christian West was using nongovernmental organizations to infiltrate the Sudan with religious and political agendas. Acknowledging the food shortages, the government feared, would trigger another international relief intervention.

The second challenge is the relationship between relief operations and long-term problems. During emergencies operational concerns quite naturally take priority. The endemic causes of the crisis—agricultural policies and political, ethnic, and religious tensions—get short shrift. The challenge is to use relief activities as an entry point for addressing matters of long-term consequence: underdevelopment, environmental degradation, human rights violations, and conflict. Relief operations need to be sensitive to their context and to try to make maximum use of local human and material resources, social structures, value systems, and survival techniques.

The OEOA at first involved few people with few resources. When food shortages began appearing in 1983–84, Sudanese authorities were slow to respond. Relief activities, after a sluggish start, mushroomed into a monumental operation that became a source of both appreciation and resentment. Within six months the emergency operation had a mammoth structure of its own, involving large numbers of expatriates, more than five hundred local support personnel, offices around the country, and a radio communications network more reliable than the national telephone system. The OEOA mobilized a fleet of almost four hundred trucks and a dozen aircraft, dwarfing the resources available to the government.

To be sure, the crisis was severe enough to justify a warlike mobilization of human and material resources to deliver food to the starving. The relief operation, however, soon took on a life of its own. One observer described the OEOA as "a top-down, heavy handed operation which was mainly interested in getting more trucks and more radios to equip the trucks with and carrying out a military-style operation with very little regard to the actual social, developmental, political . . . sides of the whole equation."

Critics also held that the international relief effort probably entrenched the causes of the famine itself. Beneficiaries had not been enlisted in the relief activities, and the strategies and technologies employed may have rendered communities more dependent on outside assistance. For example, water pumps required spare parts available only outside the Sudan, and seeds and fertilizers were imported.

When John Garang, chairman of the SPLM and commander-in-chief of the SPLA, learned in June 1991 that the airlift of food from Nairobi to Juba had cost fully $35 million during its two and a half years of operation, his response was immediate. How much better it would have been, he mused, to meet the food needs of Juba civilians in cheaper ways. Then the $1,000 per ton consumed in air transport costs could have been used instead, he said, for seeds, tools, water resources development, and education.

So urgent was the need to move supplies into remote areas that Operation Lifeline Sudan became a logistical Mission Impossible. The Khartoum conference in March 1989, which launched Lifeline, set

tonnage targets that would haunt the program. With every well-pub-
licized failure of trucks, trains, and barges to reach their destinations,
Lifeline seemed a step closer to collapse. It did not reach its end-of-
June target of 107,000 tons until October, although by year's end it
had moved some 111,654 tons of food and 3,760 tons of nonfood
items. While few people knew the nutritional capacities or physical
dimensions of a ton, many saw in Lifeline's tonnage reports an indicator—mistaken, as it turned out—of a failed undertaking. By May
1989, a consultant visiting the southern Sudan reported that an over-
emphasis on tonnages moved had "tended to create a short-term relief
mentality that obscures equally important medium-term needs and
the opportunity to provide relief in a way that supports, rather than
undercuts, longer-term development."[12]

However urgent the logistic challenges of emergency relief operations, the underlying causes of suffering must be addressed if the
assistance is to bring about a more food-secure future. In the Sudan,
this meant government attention to the causes of chronic food insecurity, including the civil war itself.

A third challenge is that of coordination. Too little coordination can
result in duplication of relief efforts, and too much can hamstring
effective operations. Despite widespread agreement on the desira-
bility of coordination, however, few relief agencies welcome the dis-
cipline that coordination imposes. Getting the balance right under
the pressure of extreme human need is not easy.

An important reason for coordination is the high cost of international relief operations. The levels of assistance were too high to be
sustained over an extended period and perhaps even too high for the
short term. The OEOA exercised the coordinating role in 1984–86,
and Operation Lifeline Sudan did the same later. The United Nations
helped alert the international community to the scale of the need,
mobilized substantial resources, assisted in the delivery of supplies,
served as liaison between aid agencies and Sudanese authorities, and
provided a basic accountability.

Nevertheless, serious problems developed. Some of the difficulties
were essentially technical, such as maintaining accurate, up-to-date,
and comparable information from each participant. Other difficulties
were political, such as efforts by the authorities, in the name of coordination, to control and constrain relief activities, on occasion using

the United Nations for that purpose. Other difficulties reflected inter-agency rivalries within the UN system. Both technical and political issues were complicated by the civil war.

The fourth challenge concerns the ambivalent results of emergency operations. When relief activities wind down and the international community moves out, the beneficiaries are supposed to be better equipped for whatever the future may bring. Relief operations often do not measure up to expectations in this respect.

Although international assistance should make political authorities more responsive to the people, it can also reinforce the inhumane practices of governments and armed opposition groups, shift the burden of civilian needs to the international community, and contribute to dependency on outside assistance.

Outside resources invested in emergency operations in sub-Saharan Africa were significantly higher in the 1980s than in the previous decade. The levels of assistance reflected an increase in conflict-generated need among major recipients such as the Sudan, Mozambique, Angola, and Ethiopia. At the same time, however, such aid may have contributed to the continuation of the strife.

"The time has come for us in the Horn of Africa," Kenyan peace activist Kibiru Kinyanjui has observed, "to ask whether the efforts of relief agencies are contributing, indirectly or even remotely, to an escalation of the wars or to a peaceful resolution of the conflicts." Lifeline's preoccupation with logistics helps account for its inattention to the conflict. On the positive side, however, Lifeline brought the war to the attention of the world and triggered efforts to find a solution.

The interplay of political realities and humanitarian objectives contributes to the mixed results of relief activities. In the drought-related crisis, the Sudan government's reluctance to acknowledge the famine was clearly political. Donor governments, in particular the United States, were perceived to be boosting the Nimeiri regime, which became an ally of the West on a number of strategic issues. Most Western donors were reluctant to press Khartoum to deal with human need when the regime was not prepared to do so. But eventually the West, led by the United States, pressured Nimeiri into declaring a state of emergency and inviting international assistance.

A humanitarian initiative, Lifeline was also highly political. "Relief is not a value-free operation," observed Abu Ouf, the Sudanese government's relief and resettlement commissioner. "It is based on the interest of the countries involved. It has a cultural and a religious dimension. It is a network of sometimes conflicting interests and forces pushing toward different goals, though dressed up in the same garb."[13]

Relief workers were understandably frustrated by the ambivalent results of the best-intended and most successful relief efforts. One interviewed in 1986 commented, "It is a puzzling type of thing—this ambivalence toward the aid that is coming in, as if they [the Sudanese] do not care. Some of our people say we should just pack it in and take it somewhere else." The dichotomy expressed between "us" and "them" was pervasive.

Less widely known was the questioning by Sudanese people themselves of the usefulness of relief efforts. One Sudanese professor lamented, "We should have been left alone." Disturbed by what he saw as an arrogant and obtrusive foreign relief community in Khartoum, he also felt that relief operations reinforced Nimeiri's regime, gave him international legitimacy, and perhaps prolonged his last days with gross violations of the very human rights he himself advocated.

Both outside and inside the Sudan, then, informed persons of compassion and conscience found themselves profoundly ambivalent about emergency operations. Aid interventions, they found, demonstrate that humanitarian initiatives, however compelling on moral grounds, exercise no compelling authority when political or military forces are otherwise inclined. In addressing one problem successfully, relief activities may also create or compound others.

At the same time, the Sudan experience suggests that humanitarian initiatives, creatively managed, can be an influential force in their own right. Interventions can be made more proportionate and precise and their side effects minimized. Costs can be contained, although relief efforts will never be cheap. If the complex motives and mixed results of humanitarian aid are acknowledged, the international community can accentuate its humanitarian purposes and achieve the best possible results for those in need.

Chapter 2

Drought-Induced Famine, 1983–86

The famine of 1983–86, which devastated Darfur, Kordofan, and the Red Sea Hills regions of the northern Sudan, was triggered by an environmental catastrophe, the failure of rains. The scores of thousands of people who starved to death did not die because the rains failed, however. They died because they were too poor to buy food when the drought prevented them from growing what they needed, and their government could not provide them with food and did not invite the international community in time to assist with the delivery and distribution of emergency supplies. The famine was a crisis of poverty and governance. The former was reflected in the lack of purchasing power, the latter in the alienation of the government from the rural poor, who did not possess the political clout to make the national authorities accountable. In other words, it was a crisis of legitimacy.

GENESIS OF THE EMERGENCY

The causes of famine are not limited to poverty and government failure to provide food when there is an acute shortage or to solicit relief from the international community. Both hunger and its roots in poverty can be attributed to a complex combination of political, economic, and environmental factors that have a negative effect on productivity, distribution, and the sustainability of life. As Nick Cater observed in a report to the humanitarian organization Oxfam on the 1983–86 famine, "Sudan's crisis has been linked, amongst other things, to the introduction of new agricultural methods, political systems and economic frameworks which damage the old ways of life and erode the network of support that existed within families, villages and tribes.

As sustainable food production is abandoned, the intricate mechanisms of survival break down and the common climate variation of drought ceases to be an endurable calamity and becomes an engulfing disaster."[1]

Interviews with the local inhabitants in the affected areas, particularly in Darfur, revealed that signs of the impending disaster were visible as early as 1982. At that time, decreasing levels of rainfall and food production began to have a serious effect on the rural population, capping a trend that had been developing for twenty years. The steady decrease in precipitation caused the desert to creep southward an average of six kilometers a year. Poor rains in 1983 followed by no rains in 1984 brought the crisis to a head.

Although the richer central regions of the Sudan were also affected, the vulnerable, poverty-stricken western and eastern regions were particularly devastated, and the classic symptoms of famine were visible even before the 1984 harvest. Livestock began to perish in large numbers. Sorghum prices soared to ten times normal levels, far beyond the purchasing power of the rural poor. In contrast, prices fell to about a tenth of the previous levels for cattle, sheep, and camels, which rapidly depleted the exchange rate of herds for the purchase of food. People began to sell more personal possessions so that they could buy food. Wage rates fell, and work eventually ran out. People resorted to gathering and eating roots, even digging termite mounds for the broken grains stored by the insects.

When people ran out of all alternative sources of food and saw no prospects for survival in their natural habitat, they began to move in massive numbers from northern Darfur, northern Kordofan, and the Red Sea Hills toward the more affluent towns and cities of El Obeid in the midwest and Omdurman, Khartoum, and Khartoum North in the center.

The dimensions of the crisis continued to expand. Oxfam surveys in Darfur and Kordofan during the early part of 1985 indicated regionwide malnutrition levels four times the African normal.[2] When rains came, disease increased. Children were said to be dying even as Oxfam was conducting the surveys.

Although travelers and relief workers were alerting the world community to the impending disaster, the government, more specifically Nimeiri himself, did not recognize, or did not want to acknowledge, that a crisis was in the making. Nimeiri's intelligence sources, known to be very efficient for political survival, must have informed him that livestock losses had gone up to between 50 percent and 70 percent in Darfur and to more than 90 percent in the Red Sea region and that people displaced by the famine were flooding to the capital. Nevertheless, other calculations or sheer indifference made Nimeiri turn a blind eye on the impending disaster.

Not until the Khartoum representative of the United States Agency for International Development (AID) decided to take up the issue did the emergency situation become a subject of discussion between the United States and the Nimeiri regime. Through the bilateral efforts of aid officials, the resident representative of the UN Development Program (UNDP) became involved but continued to be inhibited by the Sudanese official attitude, which ranged from denial to refusal to declare the emergency, even when it had become established beyond doubt.

The Sudanese crisis was aggravated but eventually brought to the attention of the world by the massive influx of refugees from its many troubled borders and especially from Ethiopia. Refugees from Ethiopia were the subjects of a dramatic BBC documentary in late 1984 that generated extensive international coverage of the Ethiopian tragedy. Even before the publicity of the Ethiopian refugee influx into the Sudan, the country was hosting three-quarters of a million refugees, half a million from Ethiopia and the rest from Uganda, most of whom were self-settled. At the beginning of 1984, 300,000 more Ethiopians fled to the Sudan, mainly from Eritrea and Tigre. By early 1985 an estimated 3,500 people were fleeing daily from the drought and the civil war in Ethiopia. On the western front, drought and insecurity drove more than 100,000 refugees from Chad into the Sudan, where they found themselves coping with the Sudanese emergency.

Despite Nimeiri's denial to the international community that famine existed in his country, the press coverage of the plight of these refugees, particularly those from Ethiopia, eventually focused the limelight on the Sudanese tragedy. Relief officials concluded that most of the population of the affected areas—anywhere from 6 million to 10 million people—were suffering.

Political tensions surrounding government policy were rising in Darfur and eventually exploded in spontaneous mass demonstrations, with the crowd crying out for food during Nimeiri's visit to El Fashir, the regional capital, in June 1984. Alarmed by the demon-

strations and fearful that Libya might exploit the situation in its conflict with Chad, Nimeiri eventually declared a state of emergency and
called for international relief assistance. The international community,
in particular USAID, responded generously and massively, posing a
coordinating challenge that naturally fell on the United Nations.

The intervention of the United Nations in the Sudanese famine and
the coordinating role it played in the emergency relief operations
should be seen in the broader context of the drought and famine that
afflicted much of sub-Saharan Africa at about the same time. The
drought that had been building up over a number of years culminated
in 1984 "in an extraordinary emergency of catastrophic proportions."[3]
Harvests failed for a third consecutive year in some countries; livestock perished in vast numbers; water levels fell to exceptionally low
levels; and severe famine, disease and death spread over some twenty
countries. Hardest hit were the rural poor, who were living at sub-
sistence levels. More than 35 million people were affected, and some
10 million left their homes in search of food and water.

Although the drought was the direct and immediate cause of declining food production, shortages, and famine, fundamentally negative economic trends had been affecting the development potential
in those countries for more than a decade. Among the causal factors
were a prolonged and widespread recession in the industrialized
countries, which diminished the flow of assistance to African countries; an increasing burden of foreign debt servicing; lower returns
from agricultural exports and other basic commodities on which the
world market prices had been falling, while the cost of imported fuel
and manufactured goods had been rising; and ecological deterioration
and demographic pressures that contributed to the socioeconomic
decline.[4]

The situation in Ethiopia worsened markedly in 1983 and 1984. The
international response was slow in coming, despite warnings by the
United Nations and nongovernmental organizations. By the end of
1984, when the media alerted the world to the tragic situation in
Ethiopia, the call for emergency relief operations echoed worldwide.

The UN secretary-general decided then to set up on a temporary
basis the Office for Emergency Operations in Africa (OEOA) to ensure
that the United Nations would respond to the emergency needs of
the affected African countries in a timely and effective manner. He
appointed as the director of the office Bradford Morse, who in turn

designated Maurice Strong as the executive coordinator. The office functioned until October 31, 1986.

The principal functions of the OEOA were to promote international coordination and cooperation in the response of the UN system to African emergency needs; to facilitate the gathering and dissemination of timely, coherent, and comprehensive information on the emergency; to assist in the mobilization of needed resources for the affected countries; and to expedite the delivery of emergency supplies by the international donor community, governmental and nongovernmental. The OEOA's information arm also maintained close regular contacts with the media, thereby helping to keep world attention focused on the African emergency.

Perhaps the least successful function of the OEOA was resource mobilization. As the secretary-general's report noted: "Donors proved to be far more responsive to needs for food aid and for logistical requirements that could be provided out of existing stocks than to the funding of critical needs for medical and health supplies, drinking water and sanitation facilities, cash for internal transport requirements and essential agricultural and pastoral inputs."[5] This observation confirms the point made earlier that a pragmatic need to utilize the accumulating food stocks in the agricultural regions of the West reinforces the humanitarian motivation for relief assistance. The situation represents a genuine convergence of interests that has long-term potential for conflict and for creative cooperation in alternative strategies for development.

Estimates of the emergency needs in 1985 resulting from the drought-induced famine in twenty African countries totaled about $3.38 billion, of which about 85 percent was provided by the end of the year. The international community organized the delivery and distribution of some 6 million metric tons of food aid during 1985. The biggest donors included the United States, Canada, and the European Community, which among them provided more than 65 percent of food relief allocations, but many countries contributed. The relief operations were truly a demonstration of global mobilization based on a heightened consciousness of one humanity. In fulfilling needs other than food, however, accomplishment remained significantly wanting throughout the emergency.[6] Some of the UN officials interviewed for the study of the drought-induced famine in the Sudan underscored this fact as one of the principal failures of the emergency operations. It remains a problem area in the global agenda on humanitarianism.

Ethiopia and the Sudan were by far the worst cases. The secretary-general appointed special representatives for both countries to discharge the functions of the OEOA at the national levels in close consultation with the host governments. Their duties were to assess the emergency requirements and priorities; to discuss them with the local representatives of bilateral programs, nongovernmental organizations, and other parties involved in the relief operations; to facilitate resource mobilization; and to coordinate collective or cooperational logistical activities in the affected areas.

At first, the resident representatives of the UNDP in the countries concerned discharged these functions. The magnitude of the Ethiopian disaster led to the appointment of a special representative of the secretary-general to enhance the authority and effectiveness of the United Nations in the emergency operations inside the country. As the situation deteriorated in the Sudan in 1984–85, Maurice Strong, the executive coordinator of the OEOA, paid a field visit in March 1985. On his return, he effected changes in the personnel that led to the transfer of Arthur Holcombe, then the resident representative, and the appointment of Winston Prattley, a veteran of other emergencies, as the secretary-general's special representative in the Sudan. The United Nations Emergency Operation for the Sudan (UNEOS) was established as the local arm of the OEOA in New York.

The Sudan became the most challenging case for the OEOA, especially in view of the political instability and the increasing magnitude of the crisis. In February 1985 the OEOA in its situation report on the Sudan noted:

A total of 4.5 million people in Darfur, northern Kordofan and the eastern region of the Red Sea province are seriously affected by the drought and have had poor harvests for four years. Food deficits are substantial. As a result, many nomadic populations have lost their crops and livestock and have moved to the southern portions of these provinces and to the Nile banks in search of relief. The problem is further compounded by the rapidly increasing influx of displaced population from drought-stricken areas of Ethiopia and Chad.

Low rainfall in the Blue Nile system has reduced crop production in the major irrigated areas of the eastern and central
regions and has eliminated winter wheat production. Grain, veg-
etable seed, livestock, draught animals and agricultural imple-
ments are required urgently. Large supplies of antibiotics and
anti-malaria, multi-vitamin and anti-dysentery drugs are required. Over 300,000 families are also in need of urgent shelter
items such as straw mats and blankets.[7]

The famine tragedy and the explosive political situation in the South
became increasingly intertwined. After Nimeiri's overthrow, the transitional government of General Abdel Rahman Siwar al-Dahab and
his civilian prime minister, Gazouli Dafalla, was cooperative. At the
same time, however, the Sudan People's Liberation Movement and
its army (SPLM-SPLA) continued the insurgency in the South. As the
transitional period gave way to the civilian rule of the sectarian political parties under Prime Minister Sadiq al-Mahdi, the war intensified. The civilian population in the South increasingly fell victim to
the conflict-related famine. The government resisted the efforts of the
United Nations to extend relief operations to the affected populations
in the South. Tensions between the prime minister and the special
representative of the secretary-general came to a head when the special representative was expelled from the Sudan as persona non grata.
North-South divisions had become obstacles not only to the delivery
of relief in the conflict-related emergency but also to the work of the
OEOA in general. The acute crisis of alienation within a nation had
become connected with the problems that generally characterize international emergency operations.

Each of the four major problems scrutinized in this study was evident during the drought-induced famine of 1983–86. External intervention was necessitated by the crisis of governance in which the
national leadership was alienated from the victim population in the
countryside. The connections between relief operations and internal
structures and processes were hampered by inadequate knowledge
of the context. Once relief activities were launched, however, they
became consuming, and other priority areas suffered neglect. Coordination was imperative, resisted by some relief agencies and the
government but imposed by the UN representative in the country.
The results of the relief operations, still debatable, left the country

and relief workers uncertain about what they had accomplished beyond saving some lives.

The emergency situation affected virtually half of the 21 million Sudanese in almost all regions of the country, not to mention the refugee community from other countries, comprising about a tenth of the total population. When cholera broke out, complicating the emergency, the central government displayed an astonishing insensitivity to the plight of its nationals. As a result, the detection, recognition, and response were delayed through critical phases and progressed only gradually as the international climate brought irresistible pressure to bear on the government to permit relief operations.

INTERVENING FROM OUTSIDE

Since international emergency relief originates outside the country, its existence implies that the national government has failed to provide for the survival of its citizens and should therefore be held accountable—if not to the citizens because of their powerlessness, then to the global community. These issues not only touch on the central values of sovereignty but also go to the heart of the national purpose and legitimacy of the government.

These factors came into focus dramatically in the Sudan. The political dimension was critical in delaying the detection of and the reaction to the emergency. While the world takes 1984 as the year when the famine broke out in the Sudan, accounts of the people in the western parts of the country, particularly Darfur, date the problem to the 1970s, when they began to notice a decline in the levels of rainfall. Experts and government authorities knew of the overall environmental degradation in the area but took no remedial measures to avert a predictable crisis.

By 1982, signs of the impending disaster were visible to travelers and field workers through the classic indicators of price fluctuation and population movement. The government of the Sudan, President Nimeiri in particular, refused to recognize the problem, declare a state of emergency, and call on the international community for assistance. The evaluation of the activities of the OEOA in Ethiopia noted a similar reluctance on the part of the authorities there to request assistance. The report recalls the belated and "woefully inadequate" efforts of the government of Emperor Hailie Selasie in the devastating famine of 1973–74 to acknowledge the need and to seek aid.[8]

The United Nations system, more specifically the Food and Agriculture Organization (FAO), alerted the world to the explosive environmental situation that was looming over Africa. After analyzing the information gathered by its Information and Early Warning System during several consecutive growing seasons, the FAO issued the first public alert in January 1983 that drought and poor harvests were causing shortages in food production and setting the stage for famine in a score of African countries.

The FAO took measures not only to ascertain the needs but also to appeal to the international community on behalf of the stricken countries. It sent missions to various parts of Africa to explore the situation further. The Sudan was not among the countries specified in the initial list. President Nimeiri, presumably aware of the efforts by the FAO, reported to FAO headquarters in Rome in November 1983 that the Sudan had been experiencing a serious drought for fifteen years. The drought had caused a loss of agricultural land in the northern parts of Darfur and Kordofan at an average rate of six kilometers a year. It is not clear whether he linked that phenomenon to any shortage of food in the country or made a specific request for aid.

Most of the credit for the efforts that eventually focused world attention on the Sudanese tragedy goes to the United States, specifically to representatives of AID in Khartoum. They not only gathered the necessary information at an early stage and continued to monitor the situation closely, but exerted pressure on the Sudanese government, specifically President Nimeiri, to recognize the problem and to seek international assistance.

The United States was motivated by both humanitarian and political considerations. The Sudan under Nimeiri had evolved into a close friend of the West and in particular of the United States. Initially, this was due to the positive domestic achievements of Nimeiri's regime. Nimeiri had ended the seventeen-year war in the South; embarked on a domestic policy oriented toward development; and promoted a domestic and a foreign policy favoring peace initiatives aimed at dialogue and negotiations toward a peaceful resolution of conflicts.

The direct result of Nimeiri's foreign policy was the Sudan's support for the Camp David accords between Egypt and Israel. Virtually all the institutions of state—the army, the intelligence apparatus, the socialist union, the ministry of foreign affairs—favored rejecting the Camp David accords. President Nimeiri, influenced by advisers who wanted to build on the positive example of the Addis Ababa agreement, chose to support the Camp David accords and to use that support as a basis for winning cooperation from the United States in particular and from the West in general. Nimeiri vacillated considerably, but the strong support he received from the United States encouraged him to maintain his stand despite the negative response of the Arab world.

This policy, combined with the geopolitical role of the Sudan as an African and an Arab country, gave the Sudan a strategic importance that considerably enhanced its potential as a moderating influence in the region and, therefore, as a worthy client for both the West and the Arab world.

In due course, however, the lofty idealism embodied in this role narrowed, becoming an ideological alignment between the West and one man, Nimeiri, because of his almost personal animosity toward the Soviet Union (after the 1976 abortive communist coup), toward Marxist Ethiopia, and toward Qadhafi's Libya and because of his daring support for Egypt. On the other hand, Nimeiri had a precarious image in the Arab world because of his support for Egypt *and* the Camp David accords, which in turn made him very close to Washington. The United States certainly wanted to save lives, and there was no question about the American desire to help a friend in need, though it did so with a gross misunderstanding of the background and dynamics of Nimeiri's political stance, which was connected with the non-Arab South and those within the regime who represented that connection.

This explains in part why most northern Sudanese could not understand, far less appreciate, Western support for Nimeiri, even in the context of the emergency relief operations. A prominent university professor and human rights advocate who was interviewed in the OEOA study argued that the link between humanitarian aid and support for the Nimeiri regime, which had become increasingly personal and unpopular, was in part responsible for the ambivalence people felt toward foreign emergency relief assistance.

Yes, relief was much welcome, was very much needed, but unfortunately it came at a time when there was a political crisis in the Sudan, when there was a dictator, when there was oppression! The drought, the famine, the refugees and finally the dictatorship became all intermingled. . . . All the facts related to famine, drought and refugees were kept secret and the Sudanese people didn't know what was happening. The Sudanese people were not told about the problem, while others were told and they came in. The political aspect became very clear to the people. Because of this association the foreign relief agencies were resented.

A prominent religious political leader who had fallen out of favor expressed it this way: "There was too much politics in the relief work. . . . The supplies were easily diverted, and there was no accountability. . . . The security people were free to deal with relief supplies. This made many people suspicious of government agencies, that they were not efficient to handle such responsibility."

The most critical issue at the early stages of the emergency remained how to move Nimeiri's government to acknowledge the problem and solicit help. Despite the efforts of AID and UN representatives in Khartoum and the evidence of malnutrition, large-scale population movements, and the threat of mass starvation, as late as mid-1984 Nimeiri refused to acknowledge that the problem was serious enough to declare an emergency.

Ahmad Ibrahim Diraige, the governor of Darfur, made repeated pleas that Nimeiri ignored. When Nimeiri refused even to see him, Diraige expressed his indignation by leaving the country, creating a dangerous vacuum in an explosive situation. Because of the sensitivity of the Sudan's border with Libya, trouble in Darfur put Nimeiri in a predicament. If he admitted the magnitude of the problem, he would be revealing domestic weakness and vulnerability. If he ignored the situation, it could explode and be exploited by a hostile neighbor unquestionably set on Nimeiri's downfall.

The United States confronted Nimeiri's dilemma by providing prompt assistance to the most vulnerable areas in the West and at the same time increasing pressure on the government to acknowledge the problem and seek international assistance. When Nimeiri was finally persuaded to visit Darfur in June 1984 because of the deteriorating political situation there and its security implications, his plane was mobbed by a crowd of demonstrators demanding food. Nimeiri declared an emergency in Darfur and ordered General Omar Mohammed al-Tayeb, first vice-president and chief of national security, to supervise food deliveries to the region. He still refused, however, to declare a national emergency.

Meanwhile, the situation in the eastern part of the country had deteriorated, aggravated by the influx of refugees and the outbreak of cholera. Nimeiri continued to deny that there was an emergency, arguing that the food shortage in the Sudan was the result of the influx of refugees and that the international donor community should indeed be assisting the refugee programs. This deflected attention from conditions in the Sudan and toward the refugees, especially the Ethiopian refugees in the eastern part of the Sudan. As a result, throughout 1984 and into early 1985, more emergency food supplies were going to refugees than to the famine-stricken Sudanese, even though observers were convinced that far larger numbers of Sudanese were affected than refugees from Ethiopia, Uganda, and, later, Chad.

The problem was compounded by the very definition of those who qualified as refugees for purposes of UN assistance. The definition covered only political refugees and not environmental refugees or those fleeing from starvation caused by forces of nature, which was the plight of the Sudanese affected by the drought. The Sudanese government and people were unusually hospitable to the refugees who poured into the country. Although the Sudanese continued to demonstrate generosity even during periods of hardship, for the government to cater to the refugees while the local population suffered and received no help was to risk causing resentment of the refugees among the local population.

During the last six months of 1985, half a million refugees poured into the Sudan from Ethiopia, Chad, and Uganda. The problem was so grave and was causing so much friction that regional authorities and even Nimeiri himself became reluctant to approve the establishment of more refugee camps.

Maurice Strong, executive coordinator of the OEOA, and his colleagues were able to make a convincing case to the UN High Commission for Refugees (UNHCR) and to the Sudanese National Commission for Refugees for providing more resources. The specialized UN agencies also responded by authorizing assistance to the victims of famine in or near refugee feeding centers, whether or not they technically qualified as refugees. The UNHCR and the World

Food Program (WFP) made no distinction between political and economic or famine refugees. They extended help to both. UN officials intimated that the high commissioner for refugees had been criticized for this flexible use of allocated resources.

When the UNHCR included Sudanese nationals in its feeding programs, Nimeiri's regime rationalized the measure on the grounds that the refugees were depleting the available national resources, rather than acknowledging that the country was suffering from a major famine and needed help. Among the explanations offered for Nimeiri's negative attitude toward the famine in his country were national and personal pride, fear of aggravating the rise in prices, and the risk of endangering the country's security.

Pride seemed misplaced in the setting of mass starvation and government helplessness, however. Prices had already increased as high as threefold in the western areas and sixfold in the Red Sea Hills. Security was already precarious; food riots had erupted in fifteen or more different towns of the North in the period between June 1984 and May 1985. In other words, there appears to be no way to exonerate the regime. The only credible explanation is that Nimeiri's objectives and concerns were isolated from those of his people and their need, indeed their struggle for survival, and that he read or misread the international climate, particularly in the West, as favoring him personally rather than the people of the Sudan as a whole. Among the politically motivated, rejecting Nimeiri became synonymous with rejecting international relief, especially from the United States, as support for the status quo.

FRAMING THE CONTEXT

Relief operations need to be undertaken with a clear understanding of the fabric of life in the country, in urban centers and rural areas alike. They need to take account of the conceptual and operational mechanisms for economic, social, and cultural life and survival techniques in times of emergency. Available information and accumulated knowledge provides the framework within which relief programs are planned and carried out.

The most crucial factor in the Sudanese case was the scarcity of information with which to predict and fight the famine. A senior UN official in the Sudan called this "the information drought." The FAO had its sophisticated Global Information and Early Warning System, but the Sudan at the outbreak of the emergency had no comparable system. Rural areas were particularly remote from any significant monitoring mechanisms. The British, during colonial times, had maintained a system of gauging the climate and weather conditions, monitoring the food situation, and preparing for any emergency. The system, though simple, was quite effective. In earlier days, the Sudanese government's meteorological department had a high profile; its long monitoring arm reached every small government post, where simple instruments for gauging the levels of rainfall were erected and carefully observed.

Various agencies and organizations such as AID, the United Nations International Children's Emergency Fund (UNICEF), the World Health Organization, and Oxfam-UK conducted nutritional and health surveys that detected aspects of the problem early. Most of the evidence on the basis of which the emergency was eventually acknowledged, however, came from personal observations of relief field workers about the conditions in the rural areas: prices of food and livestock, dietary habits, population movements, and the emaciated look of the people, all of which was remote from the government in Khartoum.

Such technologically sophisticated methods as satellite sensing seem to have played only an indirect role as a source of information and early warning in the Sudanese situation. Some nongovernmental organizations expressed frustration over the failure to use this technology, which was attributed to political sensitivities on the part of governments that were presumably suspicious of being watched from above. Although governments did not explicitly identify the sources of their information, no one doubts that such technology was used in the Sudan. The kind of information it could reveal about the specific conditions on the ground was, however, limited.

The lack of information kept the magnitude of the problem from being properly understood even by those who were deeply concerned. Surveys by UN agencies and nongovernmental organizations and informal accounts suggested the existence of severe malnutrition and even starvation, but no systematic evidence confirmed the alarming reports.

When Nimeiri visited El Fashir in June 1984 and was received by an angry mob demanding food, the UNDP resident representative became convinced that a crisis was indeed in the making. The resident representative and the representatives of the FAO and UNICEF toured the affected regions of Darfur, Kordofan, and central and eastern regions during the period from June to August 1984, meeting with government officials of the northern region to determine the extent of the problem. Their assessment of the situation revealed that about 4.5 million people were affected and that the food deficit for 1985 was likely to be about 1.2 million metric tons. This agreed with estimates by AID, which allocated 82,000 tons to be delivered in November and December, although the actual delivery and distribution were delayed by several months because of logistical problems.

The problem of information was complicated by the fact that in a country where poverty and a degree of malnutrition were the norm in many areas, precisely what constituted an alarming level was a question. Early estimates of the needs by various agencies and even by missions of the UN system were received with skepticism and viewed as inflated; developments showed that they had understated the needs. Despite the government tendency to cover up the famine, the UNDP resident representative in Khartoum began to receive requests for food aid from the central government authorities as early as December of 1983, but these requests were not sufficiently substantiated and could not therefore be acted upon with justification.

By January 1984, representatives of the FAO and WFP in Khartoum visited the western regions of Darfur and Kordofan and prepared a report with government officials. They estimated that some 78,000 tons of food aid would be required to feed an affected population of 1 million in Darfur and 500,000 in Kordofan. The resident coordinator, who had unfortunately not seen the report before it went to FAO headquarters in Rome, considered these figures too high. Rome also received the report with skepticism and decided to send another mission to the field, as a result of which the original request was slashed to a mere 12,000 tons. As a result of negotiating delays, even this modest quantity was not delivered and distributed until August and September. This was an instance in which scarcity of information, combined with poor coordination, impeded an efficient response to the developing crisis.

As a result of uncertainties about the numbers of people affected and the kind and quantities of aid needed, supplies flowed piecemeal from a variety of sources, each building on its own evaluation of the

situation. Surveys by different agencies, using different methodolo-
gies, revealed discrepancies in the data and in its interpretation, which
in turn affected not only the amounts of food supplied but also the
manner in which the food was distributed.

The companion evaluation on Ethiopia, while giving the OEOA
and the government's Relief and Rehabilitation Commission credit
for monitoring the extent of food shortages and malnutrition, notes
that effective resource mobilization was undercut by conflicting data
from different units within the United Nations and between the United
Nations and individual donor governments.[9]

In the Sudan the dissemination of information was as critical as its
availability. Even the scanty information available was not adequately
used to mobilize the necessary response. Representatives of the UN
system tried to pass on their field findings to the national press, but
they found no response. At least initially, the international press
seemed too preoccupied with the Ethiopian famine and the refugee
situation to be concerned with the Sudan, which was in any case more
obscure and less exposed because of the government's policy of stone-
walling. As one representative of a nongovernmental organization
recalled, "It really was an awful period for us, a period of total frustration." Ironically, the Ethiopian situation and attendant refugee
problems, which initially seemed to divert attention from the Sudan,
eventually spilled over into the Sudan, highlighting the plight of the
Sudanese.

The experience of the Sudanese emergency dramatizes, therefore,
not only the crucial importance of information but also the need to
make it available to the concerned participants, both nationally and
internationally. The role later played by nongovernmental organizations and other field workers in monitoring the situation and by the
UN Emergency Operation for the Sudan in processing the information
and making it available to the wide circle of donors and participants
also indicates how much can be done at a minimum cost even with
rudimentary techniques.

The problem of context goes beyond the availability and dissemination of information. Also needed is a fuller understanding of the
local situation in which relief operations are set—its productive capacity, survival mechanisms, and the ability to absorb emergency
relief operations to resuscitate the system through rehabilitation and
continuing development efforts. The critical issue then becomes the

pervasive effect of massive logistical operations—whether they undermine the local economy and social and cultural fabric or reinforce them to enhance the capacity for survival and empowerment to meet future exigencies.

COORDINATING ACTIVITIES

Coordination is generally recognized as essential for the coherence and effectiveness of emergency relief operations. Donors and nongovernmental organizations resent and resist coordination, seeing it as a time-consuming, bureaucratic impediment to speedy action. The problem is that while coordination may facilitate concerted action, it can also impede relief efforts.

The need for coordination and the resistance to it were among the most controversial issues in the emergency operations during the period of drought-induced famine. Despite the earlier experience of famine in the Sahel or in Ethiopia, the Sudan was caught without an organization akin to the Relief and Rehabilitation Commission in Addis Ababa. Until UNEOS was established, there was no organizational preparedness for relief activities. Once UNEOS had assumed the role, the wide array of organizations and participants was resistant to coordination by the secretary-general's special representative in Khartoum.

Committees were created in an ad hoc reaction to the Sudan crisis. These included the Darfur Relief Committee, which Nimeiri set up after his visit to El Fashir, and the Drought and Desertification Commission, which operated under the aegis of the Ministry of Health. According to the UN coordinator, the Drought and Desertification Commission was not effective in any sense of the word. A senior official of the Ministry of Finance and National Planning noted that "the only minister who was excluded from that committee was the minister of Finance. That in itself showed how people work in this country."

After Nimeiri's overthrow, this commission continued first under the chairmanship of the head of state, the chairman of the Transitional Military Council. The Commission for Relief and Rehabilitation was then formed under the chairmanship of the prime minister. At the same time, a committee was established at a lower bureaucratic level under the auspices of the Ministry of Foreign Affairs to coordinate relations with the foreign donor community. The high profile of the commission headed by the prime minister demonstrated most effectively the priority the government gave relief work, but the need for coordinating the flood of international contributions remained unmet.

The United Nations had pressed for the establishment of a Commission for Relief and Rehabilitation, envisioning a body that would have representatives from all ministries that had connections with and responsibility for relief and rehabilitation programs. When the commission was set up as an autonomous body answerable to the prime minister, it suffered from lack of strong leadership, poor staffing, meager resources, preoccupation with personal interests, and interdepartmental rivalries.

The Ministry of Health continued to play a significant role in coordinating the programs and activities of international donors and nongovernmental organizations that related to health matters. The Ministry of Planning and its Food Aid National Administration (FANA) felt that it should have been given the functions of the Commission for Relief and Rehabilitation, which merely duplicated the work of other agencies. As a result of these interdepartmental differences, no coordination existed between the FANA and the commission. Their differences were accentuated by the fact that planning authorities considered rehabilitation an aspect of development that should fall under their jurisdiction.

At the end of the transitional period, a new commissioner with more political clout was appointed. Presumably to allay the fears of other departments and ministries, he immediately stressed cooperation and prudently tried to play down his political weight and high profile, but he could not transcend his partisan or political base of power, and the commission remained highly politicized.

International groups, unlike the agencies inside the Sudan, recognized from the start that coordination was critical for gathering and disseminating information and mobilizing support for relief operations. The creation of the OEOA in late 1984 had addressed this issue. As mentioned earlier, the OEOA's functions included evaluating and communicating information to the international community; serving as a clearing-house for coordinated responses to questions on the emergency; ensuring the continued cooperation of donor and recipient governments; and providing operational liaison with affected governments, UN field offices, and nongovernmental organizations.

When the OEOA was founded, there was no doubt about the urgent need for a more coordinated relief operation. The UNHCR was then the only UN agency equipped to work with emergencies, but its mandate was restricted to crises with political and not natural causes. The United Nations Disaster Relief Office (UNDRO) seemed to be the most appropriate agency, but it proved unequal to dealing with the support problems that arose not only in the Sudan but in the famine emergency throughout the continent. Beyond their areas of specialization, the UN organizations had a "pitiful lack of coordination." The OEOA was created to function in a rather unconventional way under the leadership of two outstanding personalities, Bradford Morse as the director and Maurice Strong as the executive coordinator.

Some people argue that the OEOA succeeded in spite of the UN system. Others see it as evidence not only of what the United Nations does in fact do, but also of the considerable potential that exists within the system. To the extent that this potential was at least in part tapped with unusual, if not unprecedented, success, the OEOA must be taken as a success story for which the credit lies both within and beyond the system and as an indication of what individuals can do as well as of what is possible when the UN system and outside partners cooperate.

The OEOA was established because influential personalities within the UN system felt that the situation called for a coordinating body that would be recognized and respected by the large UN agencies and the major donors, such as the United States and the European Community.[10]

The specific mandate of the OEOA was to assist the secretary-general "to ensure that all elements directly responsible to him as Secretary-General work together with the highest degree of effectiveness and harmony in bringing to bear their respective competence in assisting the African countries which are being so severely affected in meeting the emergency situation" and "in ensuring effective coordination of the assistance and support of the United Nations for these African countries which have been so cruelly and tragically affected by catastrophic drought and famine." In order to respond to this mandate, the OEOA strove from the start of its operations to develop a management structure and mode of operation aimed at maximizing a collaborative, problem-solving capability that became known as the Africa Emergency Response System.

The system functioned on four interrelated levels. The first comprised executive directors of the UN organizations that were most involved in the relief efforts—UNDP, UNHCR, UNICEF, and WFP. They consulted with the OEOA's director and executive coordinator to provide overall policy guidance.

The second level was a small secretariat at the UN headquarters in New York. In addition to the director and the executive coordinator, it had four operational units: field liaison and operations; monitoring and evaluation; public information and external relations; and liaison with nongovernmental organizations and the private sector.

The third level was represented by the Emergency Operations Group, chaired by the resident coordinators in each of the affected countries, or, in the case of Ethiopia and the Sudan, by the special representatives of the secretary-general and representatives of concerned UN agencies. Their task was to coordinate with the host government, representatives of the donor community, and nongovernmental organizations. With the involvement of other UN technical agencies concerned, such as the World Health Organization and the FAO, the Emergency Operations Group also functioned as an instrument for gathering and processing information on the emergency assistance requirements at the field level. This information was then forwarded to the OEOA headquarters in New York for further processing by the agency representatives and, if necessary, verified by government and field representatives before it was finalized and included in the OEOA's monthly status reports and in other statements of emergency needs.

Also vital to emergency operations, though not officially an organ of the OEOA administrative structure, was the African Emergency Task Force, which included high-level representatives of the UN organizations and agencies concerned. Chaired by Charles LaMunière, the deputy executive coordinator, the task force provided a critical forum in which OEOA policies were discussed, refined, and translated into operational directives, or, conversely, where practical problems from field operations could be addressed and resolved.

The structure and the principles that governed the operation of the OEOA brought together agencies for whom the overriding objective was the urgent provision of emergency requirements to a stricken population. To OEOA sources,

> this translated, *inter alia*, into a consistent drive towards the emergency provision of timely and credible information to the donor community (as an essential tool of resource mobilization efforts);

the use of eminently pragmatic and speedy solutions to urgent problems even if this implied departing from rules and procedures; the setting aside of traditional agency interests in response to the overriding shared goal of increased efficiency in responding to the needs of the affected countries and, concomitantly, the acceptance of an agreed and simplified definition of responsibility allowing the UN organizations concerned to concentrate on the facets of the emergency for which they were best equipped to deal with.[11]

The pivotal factor in this cooperation within the UN system was the example that the leaders of the agencies set for their organs and staff. Beyond the UN system, this functional cooperation at the leadership level extended to the working relationships between the director and the executive coordinator of the OEOA and the senior officials of the major donor governments. Communications were frequent when logistical bottlenecks threatened the delivery and distribution of urgently needed supplies.

The network of these high-level contacts extended from New York to Washington and across the Atlantic to the capitals of the European donors, not to mention the UN representatives and government circles in Khartoum. At times, even a donor as pivotal as AID requested the UN leadership to intervene with the government to facilitate a certain line of policy or action. One example was the need for Sudan government intervention with the Sudan railway authorities to move supplies that were not getting through.

Another critical factor in the OEOA's success was the establishment at the OEOA of an effective system of information gathering with a dynamic unit for its dissemination that was a vital link with media in stimulating an international response to the African emergency. Equally pivotal was the OEOA's recognition of the importance of the private sector and in particular of the nongovernmental organizations and popular movements, reflected in the establishment of a special unit to handle relationships with them.

The OEOA achieved its goals and operational principles of coordination and cooperation only after considerable difficulties. The role of the United Nations, initially conducted through informal meetings with field agencies and constrained by the negative attitude of the Sudan government, began to gain momentum with the creation of the OEOA and the positive response of the world community. The need for coordinating relief operations inside the Sudan became pressing as the response mounted.

The involvement of the donor community increased significantly. At one point some 160 nongovernmental organizations were involved in relief work in the Sudan. Many of these were not even officially registered. The popular perception was that no one knew who was doing what, where, or through whom. UNEOS was created to meet that need. With its creation, the UN representative in Khartoum had to assert a coordinating leadership. The reaction to this assertiveness constituted a coordination problem.

As noted earlier, one of the remarkable features of the African emergency was the crucial and indeed heroic role individuals played in coordinating the massive involvement of the world community. In Ethiopia, Kurt Janssen's personality and abilities made him remarkably successful under most trying circumstances, a level of accomplishment that was effectively sustained by his successor, Michael Priestley. In the Sudan, Arthur Holcombe, UNDP resident representative and coordinator of the UN system from mid-1984 to mid-1985, and Winston Prattley, who replaced him and was appointed special representative of the secretary-general, made remarkable contributions to the relief effort.

Holcombe found himself at the brink of a national catastrophe that Nimeiri's regime obstinately refused to acknowledge. Holcombe and his UN colleagues—operating under the constraint that UN agencies can act only with the agreement of the host government—worked tirelessly to change the situation through meetings with government officials and representatives of foreign governments.

Winston Prattley, special representative of the secretary-general, brought to the situation a practical and forceful management style, which made him both effective and controversial. The reaction of the UN system and the donor community to coordination in general and to the role of Prattley in particular ranged from unqualified praise to unmitigated criticism. The UN system and the agencies within it have a reputation of being autonomous and resistant to coordination; donor institutions, governmental and nongovernmental, are so independent as to be hostile to the very notion of coordination. The main office of the OEOA in New York functioned on the basis of a committee system, with the chairman as a leader among peers, an approach many felt was impractical under the emergency conditions at the field level.

In Ethiopia, although Kurt Janssen was the special representative of the secretary-general in charge of emergency operations, he was not involved in the normal functions of the UNDP resident representative and resident coordinator of the UN system. In principle this arrangement might have created a schism, but Janssen was able to avoid it. The United Nations wanted to change that situation by making the special representative of the secretary-general in the Sudan the head of both the emergency operation and the UN developmental system. This dual responsibility was expected to result in enhanced coordination, cohesiveness, and effectiveness—a replication of the teamwork that functioned effectively at the headquarters. Prattley, however, chose to make his role and that of UNEOS more operational and integrational than had previously been the practice within the UN system. As Prattley himself argued, "The major issue is one of operational command and effectiveness."

In more precise terms, the task force system Prattley envisaged would function in the manner described by a UN official in the Sudan:

> Task force cooperation, as it is set up at OEOA, meant that each organization kept its distinct responsibilities for particular sectors. One organization may say "We will be able to take care of health and nutrition." Another would say, "We will be able to take care of development linked with relief." World Food Programme, for instance, would take care of food distribution. Each one would forget who the other players in this whole thing were after nominal discussions on how to coordinate. . . .
>
> The operational structure design meant that one person, Mr. Prattley, was responsible. The staff of the various organizations would then collaborate to get the job done. But it is very clear that they would be in line in their relationship with the government through Mr. Prattley. In a relief situation, you almost have to work in a military fashion because if it becomes a matter of talking and disagreeing and then some people say "Well, I can do anything I want because I'm independent," you eventually are going to lose lives. And you simply should not do that from any point of view.

Perhaps the person most critical of Prattley's approach was the representative of UNICEF, who had served for a relatively long time in the country and whose agency had been one of the most active and efficient in the field. He reasoned that the Geneva Conference in 1985 had given his agency a coordinating role in the fields of health, water, shelter, and supplementary feeding and that Prattley's plans to establish his own team in those fields and in agriculture was a contravention of that mandate and a duplication of the work of other UN agencies.

Other differences related to such matters as the distribution of food, the sources and methods for identifying needs, and what the UNICEF representative saw as the tendency of Prattley's deputy to depend for information more on nongovernmental organizations than on the UN agencies. The strengths of the personalities involved and the lack of a clearly unified directive from the United Nations to all its agencies left the field wide open for competitiveness.

Another agency with which Prattley came into conflict was UNDRO, which was on the scene of the emergency quite early but whose role remained limited and overall impact largely insignificant. The main achievement with which it is associated, if not credited, is the establishment of the United Nations Relief Information Coordination Support Unit, of which Prattley was critical. When Prattley suggested that all its activities be coordinated and assimilated under the auspices of UNEOS, UNDRO objected. Although in the end Prattley persuaded UNDRO to cooperate, its involvement with the Sudanese emergency was short lived.

UNDRO must have been frustrated by a combination of factors, some of which were inherent in the difficult emergency situation. For an agency that specializes in disaster relief, however, UNDRO's performance in the Sudanese emergency left much to be desired. Whether this was the result of difficulties in the working relationships or of lack of resources or capacity remains unclear. This aspect warrants closer examination for the future of UNDRO in emergency situations.[12]

Prattley also found himself in sharp confrontation with the representative of AID, Bob Brown, who is generally remembered as having been a most effective operator not only in bringing in massive U.S. contributions, but also in overcoming the regime's resistance to acknowledging the existence of the problem and appealing for foreign assistance. Two issues were central to the differences between Prattley and Brown. One had to do with the transportation of food to the West. The United States preferred to use the private sector and had contracted with a U.S.-Sudanese company, Arkell-Talab. The contract gave the company a monopoly and inflated the cost of transportation. The second issue concerned U.S. reliance on the railroad. Prattley favored diversification, especially because of the railroad's known deficiencies.

These controversies emphasize the difficulties facing the UN coordinator, even in his capacity as special representative of the secretary-general, in coordinating activities. This was especially difficult with AID, by far the most generous agency involved with the Sudan relief operations. The problems of coordination also involved relations with European donors and touched on critical issues of supply and transportation.

These were only a few of the many situations in which UNEOS under Prattley found itself squeezed between the Sudanese government and major donors. Indeed, because the government did not have an effective national body to coordinate with the donors, UNEOS found itself in the complex and sensitive position of mediator between the government and the donors. The general feeling was that while both governmental and nongovernmental organizations appreciated whatever information they obtained as to where they might fruitfully invest their resources and energies, they did not want to be coordinated in a way that might subordinate their objectives or modes of operation to the dictates of another organization or individual.

Virtually all the people interviewed testified that in retrospect, Prattley had done a remarkable job under difficult and trying circumstances. Prattley himself concluded that the required coordination dissipates too much energy that could be more constructively spent on mobilization, delivery, and distribution of emergency supplies. The effectiveness of such a broad-based emergency operation requires some central direction and coordination of activities to avoid duplication and even conflict in the operations. Perhaps the issue is a choice between different modes of coordination, of which the OEOA and the Prattley models are examples. With time and experience, Prattley's model moved more toward the OEOA model applied in New York.

As it evolved, the coordinating role of UNEOS involved organizing monthly aid-coordinating meetings attended by the Commission for Relief and Rehabilitation, the UN agencies, diplomatic missions, and nongovernmental organizations to assess needs and pledges, to coordinate the contributions and activities of various donors and operational agencies, and to discuss other issues pertinent to the emergency. Smaller meetings, at which important logistical, resource-availability, conservation, and other policy matters were considered, were also held regularly with key donors. UNEOS also prepared weekly and monthly reports about the deteriorating situation in the South and published an early warning system bulletin.

From the beginning, relief work in the Sudan was conducted according to a geographical division of labor agreed to among the major donors and the distributing agencies. The United States assumed the major responsibility for the West, Darfur, and Kordofan, while the rest of the donors, especially the European Community and Canada, took care of the main requirements of the other northern regions. The distribution of food was carried out in Darfur principally by Save the Children–United Kingdom; in Kordofan by CARE and Save the Children–United States; in the central regions of the Blue Nile by World Vision and WFP; in Kassala by CARE; and in the Red Sea Hills by Oxfam-UK and WFP, which also took charge of the province.

Although the Sudanese government and the major donors agreed on this arrangement, it was severely attacked by Sudanese spokesmen of a Muslim relief agency for its divisiveness. As one of them explained, "This arrangement entails that if you have business in Kordofan relating to relief, you have to contact and ask CARE. Our viewpoint in relation to the balkanization of the Sudan into areas of influence is that it is unfair and uncalled for. We as an African and Islamic organization do not recognize it as binding on us as far as our operations are concerned."

Initially, the funding for the distribution of food was channeled through the World Food Program's Management and Logistics Team (MALT), which was established in July 1984 with the assistance of the Dutch government. MALT and the Road Transport Organization (RTO) provided UNEOS with a logistical operating arm. When the major donors seemed dissatisfied with official channels, they directed their resources through private allied agencies. "Unfortunately," according to one UN source, "this created a lot of confusion as to who was doing what and where, especially as there was at that time still no adequate coordination." Whatever coordinating role the UN offered could be effective only if the nongovernmental organizations wanted it. "Of course, they had their own obligations to the people in their countries on whom they were dependent."

As noted earlier, donors were more generous in their response to the UN call for emergency assistance with supplies from their stocks of food than they were with financial contributions. In the Sudan, the diversion of financial resources from the UN channels of distribution to nongovernmental organizations compounded the problems facing UN relief operations, creating an acute shortage of funds. Speaking of the situation in 1985, one UN official said, "Our problems revolved almost entirely around money. We simply could not raise the money we needed. That was something that nobody here could understand after the clear message around the world that an almost unlimited amount of money was available for Ethiopia and the Sudan. The Geneva meeting had pledged one and a half billion dollars for relief, but we could not get hold of a few thousand at times."

The implications of money shortages were dramatic. A relief worker explained:

> Sometimes, the whole operation was hampered because of lack of money. . . . We wonder that we succeeded at all, because we had to take many risks by just starting transport without any money, hoping the money would come in time to pay the transporter. We had troubles because the drivers in the smaller transporters came to our offices in Port Sudan and met us with knives. The common way of doing business here is that if a driver comes back with a signed label, he gets the money. We had bigger transporters who were supposed to be the ones dealing with us, but if they hadn't got the money, then the drivers came to our offices because they knew it came from the United Nations.

The acute shortage of cash available to the UN operations should not, of course, be generalized to the whole emergency operation, since the major donors were making the financial means for delivery and distribution of relief supplies directly available to their national nongovernmental organizations, which were doing much of the work on the ground.

Despite these early constraints, the role of the United Nations in coordinating international relief activities gained momentum as all concerned developed a mutually acceptable mode of operation. As time went by, UNEOS came to play a vitally important role in the emergency, a level of success that can be appreciated best if contrasted with the chaotic situation that had prevailed earlier. The fact that valuable time and energies were initially dissipated in fights within the UN system and with other donors is itself a lesson from which to learn. That Prattley was apparently able to overcome those difficulties is also a lesson in mutual accommodation.

In retrospect, it seems that at first everyone relied too much on the one man at the top—the special representative of the secretary-general. Prattley himself argued that although he had always thought that detecting capabilities and delegating responsibilities were among his "talents," he was unable to do that in the Sudan, not because the right people did not exist but because they apparently did not want to go to the Sudan. The problem was not unique to UNEOS. The staffs of the nongovernmental organizations also had little continuity. "I came in May 1985," explained one representative in 1986. "Right now I think I am the third longest serving director among the NGOs." Such problems within the staffs of relief organizations, nongovernmental and governmental alike, suggest fundamental problems in the area of recruitment for emergency operations. This often led to grabbing any expatriate who happened to be within easy reach and available. The level of expertise these people brought to the job was often significantly wanting. Their salaries and lifestyles as expatriates were conspicuously better than those of Sudanese of much higher qualifications, a situation that inevitably increased bitterness and ambivalence toward the foreign workers and relief operations in general.

Emergency operations in Ethiopia were generally smoother and more successful. The government's relief agency had been in existence since the major famine of the previous decade and had more operational capacity and political clout within the government. Better organization in the donor and NGO communities in Addis Ababa also made a positive contribution. The OEOA, working with its counterpart Office for Emergency Operations in Ethiopia (OEOE), is credited with coordinating a relief program that was "a great success insofar as it was very probably the main factor in keeping between seven and eight million people alive."[13]

One lesson to be drawn from the Sudanese experience is that while coordination is essential to relief operations, it is also potentially an obstacle to achieving the very objective it is meant to promote. It therefore requires careful management to minimize negative competition and rivalry and to foster harmony and mutual cooperation among the donors and field operators.

EVALUATING THE RESULTS

There is a basic irony in relief operations. They compensate for the failure of the national system to provide a remedy for the breakdown of normal survival mechanisms. In doing so, however, they discredit the system and orient recipients toward external sources of support that ultimately undermine self-reliance and encourage dependency. The critical question in evaluating results is, therefore, whether emergency relief operations reinforce local and national mechanisms for survival and self-sustaining development or undermine indigenous values, institutions, and social organization around which the local population has structured and developed strategies for combating emergencies.

If poverty and underdevelopment are the causes of famine, then eliminating them is the remedy. That means channeling resources properly toward development. Aspects of the emergency situation relating to poverty and underdevelopment fall into four categories: indigenous resourcefulness and survival capability; infrastructure and logistical constraints; food assistance and the tendency toward dependence on it; and the relationship among relief, recovery, and development activities.

Indigenous Capabilities

Indigenous resourcefulness and survival capability are revealed not only in the people's techniques for storing food but also in the creative ways in which they combat famine during times of acute shortages. Local communities in the Sudan, and indeed elsewhere in most of Africa, have a wide variety of ways of storing food. The colonial system recognized, encouraged, and supplemented these with modern storage of substantial strategic food reserves for hard times when government intervention with food assistance might be necessary. During the 1983–86 crisis, by the time the government had shipped 21,500 tons of sorghum to the western regions, only 18,750 tons remained in the strategic grain reserves, which everyone acknowledged had been grossly neglected since independence.

Resourcefulness went beyond the storage capacity of individual families or even the state. The manipulation of the market and especially the hoarding of grain by local traders contributed significantly to the dynamics of the emergency. The question might indeed be posed whether there was in fact a nationwide shortage of grain or whether the scarcity was created by hoarding and by the difficulties of moving grain from surplus to deficit areas.

If the shortages were debatable with respect to the situation in 1985, by 1986 the problem had shifted from one of nationwide shortage to that of local deficits. The challenge for relief workers was to make cash available for purchases from the surplus of about a million tons of local grain and to move the grain to areas where the deficit was estimated to be in the range of 300,000 to 500,000 tons. The leaders of UN emergency operations had to persuade donors *not* to contribute food, which would depress the prices for producers, but rather to contribute cash to purchase and transport grain for the needy, which would also provide producer incentives. Two-thirds of the required amount of cash was provided by the United States.

By June 1985 food deliveries were reported to be down to less than 15 percent of daily requirements for the most urgent needs. By that time, the international community had moved not more than a quarter of its tonnage target westward. Field workers predicted that the disaster was "already too far advanced to be contained without significant loss of lives," grimly estimated by some to be in the range of 100,000 by the end of the year in the most optimistic scenario. They reported that at least 20,000 more children were dying every month than would normally die. Observers were predicting mass starvation that might result in the death of about half a million people in the western areas of the Sudan alone.

In Ethiopia, too, a heavy price was paid for the slowness of the international response. The OEOA evaluation report concluded:

> The emergency organizational decisions could and should have come earlier than they did. Had they been taken one year, or even half a year earlier, and had they been coupled with a resource mobilization by bilateral donors not too far off the mark actually attained in late 1984 and early 1985, then additional lives, tens or hundreds of thousands, would have been saved, and at a lower cost than the one incurred.[14]

Most observers agree that many of the deaths anticipated in the Sudan did not actually occur. The most dramatic aspect of indigenous resourcefulness during the emergency situation was the ability of the people to resort to time-honored survival techniques. Although these were crude and unacceptable by minimum global standards of human dignity, they nevertheless enabled hundreds of thousands and perhaps millions to withstand the onslaught of the famine disaster. As the UN resident coordinator and UNDP resident representative at the time put it:

> Many people concluded that it was, more than anything else, a tribute to the people themselves that they could survive during this period between April or May through November 1985 with the new harvest. The fact that people turned to traditional wild foods and otherwise kept themselves going—tapping roots, leaves, insects, and other nutrients available to them—is more due to their resourcefulness and ability to survive than the capacity of the international donor community.

Some observers still wonder what might have happened if the international relief operations had not been carried out. They speculate that mass migration would have taken place, with severe problems for the migrants, and there would certainly have been much suffering and considerable loss of life, but that the level at which people were dying would probably have been lower than was assumed.

The world probably would not tolerate the forms of survival that were acceptable in the past, however. Notions of development have overtaken mere survival. As a senior United Nations official put it, "I don't know that survival on insects is development—it's survival in one way or another. The advantage of relief over some form of survival by eating the berries is that relief can be used as a tool to stimulate development."

Since the long-term objective is the reduced vulnerability of the rural population, building on the resourcefulness and potential of the people ought to be a matter of special interest to all donors. One of the most disturbing features of the emergency situation in the Sudan, however, was the extent to which mass dislocation had resulted in a sudden explosion of the urban population. Large numbers of destitute people were living in appalling, crowded conditions on the periphery of the cities.

It was by no means certain that most of these people would ever return to their villages, especially because security conditions in many rural areas eventually allowed virtually no alternative to displacement. As Prattley observed, these clusters of urban immigrants represent a "time bomb" that must be defused by meeting essential needs urgently, lest a devastating explosion become inevitable. The Sudanese emergency resulted in a sudden coming together of the village and the city in a way that challenged conventional development theories about rural-urban dichotomies. This set the stage for both conflict and cooperation between rural and urban populations.

Infrastructure

Infrastructure is another area of the relief operations program that may seem to have ambivalent results. The critical problems of transportation and the bottlenecks involved therein materialized early. The Dutch government donated logistics experts and provided them with facilities leading to the formation in July 1984 of WFP's Management and Logistics Team. This group and the UNEOS Road Transport Organization became the logistics tools of the UN operations.

While the situation in the East, with a good system of all-weather roads, was relatively secure, the western part of the country was in a vulnerable position. AID favored the private sector over public management of the transportation system and gave two contracts to Arkell-Talab, a U.S.-Sudanese joint enterprise. The first, for moving 82,000 tons of sorghum to the western part of the country, was executed smoothly. The second contract, concluded in April 1985, for taking 250,000 tons to the West before the roads became impassable with the rains, was less successful. The sorghum was transported by truck to Kosti, where there were good roads. Beyond Kosti, the company preferred to use the railroad, a decision AID endorsed. The railroad, however, had deteriorated to an appalling degree in both physical condition and management. The timing of this contract coincided with the Muslim fasting of Ramadan, when the demand for sugar was at its peak throughout the country. The railway authorities were more interested in the delivery of sugar and other items required for the traditional breakfast of Ramadan, a lopsided arrangement demonstrating that feeding the starving poor was the lowest priority. Considerable quantities of grain were lost in the delivery, and the operation was brought to a standstill when portions of the railroad were washed away by the rains.

European plans to restore the railroad system had been stalled by internal rivalries over the choice of contractor. By the time the work started, the rainy season had already begun. Although the roads were also affected by the rains, trucks offered a viable alternative to the railroad and an important means of diversifying the transportation market. In the face of this logistical breakdown, all the major participants, including AID, needed the United Nations to assist in mobilizing and coordinating alternatives. Again, high-level lines of approach involving the special representative of the secretary-general, the leadership of OEOA headquarters, and the head offices of the principal donors were brought to the front.

At this desperate juncture the European Community realized the magnitude of the crisis and began an airlift in May. But even with the EC airbridge, only a relatively small fraction of the basic and most urgent needs of the population could be satisfied. More intensive efforts were also exerted toward mobilizing a trucking fleet, but these efforts were themselves fraught with considerable difficulties. OEOA leadership in New York approached the Italians to contribute sixty trucks and thirty trailers with spare parts and mobile workshops. The EC was invited to assist in establishing a transportation task force. Using the Italian contribution as a core, UNEOS hoped to attract as many as 300 other trucks from various sources. Save the Children–UK ordered sixty trucks but assumed that they would be delivered with bodies, which, as a general practice, were locally produced. This delayed their usefulness until September, an experience that prompted a representative of Save the Children to say that "as an organization, we have learned a great number of lessons; one is to avoid this logistic business and leave that to experts, which we are not." The British-based organization Band Aid contributed about fifty second-hand trucks, electing to do this rather than import new ones partly to break the local truck cartel. Those trucks, too, were slow in arriving.

Persuaded in favor of transportation diversification and the use of trucks, AID decided to provide local currency to lease four hundred trucks to be put at the disposal of WFP. WFP's fleet became well stocked as trucks poured in from all over—Italy, Save the Children–UK, Band Aid, Germany, the United States, and the European Community. An additional one hundred trucks donated by Germany came in through the Cameroon. The Libyans dramatically overcame the challenge of logistics by crossing 1,400 miles of desert with forty-three trucks and trailers carrying supplies of grain and dried milk, escorted by a military convoy that generated considerable sensation, both locally and internationally. AID also made available three Hercules helicopters, provided ten locomotives for the railroad, and engaged a Dutch road construction team. At last, food began to flow smoothly, and about one and a half million tons were delivered to the needy in 1985.

This dramatic delivery of food, at a basic survival level that contrasted with the magnitude of the operation, indicates the manner in which the need for results overwhelms the system. The massive logistical onslaught advertised the level of assistance that was coming or was expected to come from the outside world. What was the likely effect of such demonstrations?

If the self-reliance of remote rural communities offers a useful lesson, it is that a system exists in those areas. The system has its own organizational structure and operational mechanisms that may be affected by external food aid in either of two ways. The system may be undermined and distorted into complacency and dependency on handouts, or it may be tapped as a vital resource, not only for emergencies but also for rehabilitation and development. Observers on the emergency scene have acknowledged both tendencies and potentials. Emergency relief operations had both effects.

Food Assistance

The issue of local dependency on food aid has become a topic of discussion among those concerned with relief operations. Some argue that people do not have an inherent tendency toward dependency; most people would rather work to earn a living. Others believe that people cannot resist developing a sense of dependency if they receive food for nothing. As one UN relief worker put it: "People go back to their own mechanisms for survival very rapidly, once the free assistance is withdrawn, but whilst it is there, they do take advantage of it and would be foolish not to."

The problem is aggravated when the criteria for food distribution are broad enough to cover the entire population of a village. This in itself was a point of controversy among UN agencies, with some on the scene arguing that food was going to far more people than was justified by need. The controversy arose because two methods were used to determine the levels of malnutrition and the numbers of those affected. One was the ratio of weight to height, the other the measurement of the circumference of the upper arm, mainly of children under five years old. The results differed considerably.

One senior official of a UN agency, pointing out the difference even within the UN system, noted, "We knew that there were about two million people that needed food aid, but food aid was currently going to about seven million people." Asked whether he thought food went to the people who needed it, another official who was directly involved with the distribution observed that it was very hard to give a precise answer, especially because need was not easy to determine precisely. Those interviewed generally felt that by and large the people who needed food received it. At the same time, however, many people who did not need food aid also received it.

A tribal leader in eastern Sudan told UN officials that they should "stop this whole bloody business before the people are too lazy to go to work and harvest because they are getting food for free." Some of this criticism is attributed to the influence of traders whose business interests might have been affected by food aid. Nevertheless, "one of the survival mechanisms in the Sudan," as one UN official put it, "was always migrant labor going from one area to another getting money and investing it in seeds, animals and so on. This was breaking down because of the widespread availability of food aid." That same official asked a tribal leader why his people were not moving for migrant labor and his response was "Why should they move when you *Khawajat* [Europeans] are doing such a wonderful job in giving us free food? You are doing more for us than the government has ever done before."

A highly placed official in Darfur, who saw the free distribution of food as a source of liberation for his people, remarked to a UN official that he was "delighted that his people are not going to the Gezira to collect cotton because they have been used all these centuries as slaves and now they are remaining in their own region, thanks to food aid." The special representative of the secretary-general evidently felt that there was ground for concern when he raised this striking rhetorical question: "Was that generosity—the response that came as a consequence—really the best thing for the people? Did it not evoke a response, a massive response, that might have a crippling rather than a curative effect?"

In one of the villages outside El Fashir, the people complained that there had been no food distribution for a rather long period. Since the quantities they had received when there was a distribution could not have sustained the village community with everybody in the village receiving food aid, some people were asked how they were managing on such small quantities for such lengths of time if they had no alternative sources. Their response, prefaced with laughter, was understandably evasive.

In another village, the people were unwilling to discuss the food situation. The villagers explained that the head man, who normally spoke for them, was away. Those who were there even claimed that they came from another village and could not therefore comment on the situation. The village had obviously worked out a system of communication on the emergency food supply. The villagers would risk getting in trouble with their leaders and fellow villagers if they said anything that might be interpreted as harmful to the interest of the community. A pattern of community response to food aid had already evolved that indicated a degree of manipulation that clearly went beyond dire need.

In the opinion of some, the very nature of food aid as an external input, operating above or aside from the local structures, might indeed have undermined the existing systems and aggravated the vulnerability of the people. A representative of a nongovernmental organization that had considerable experience with development at the local level over the years argued that the international relief effort probably had entrenched the very causes of the famine disaster, even though it also had saved many lives. To the degree that the beneficiaries were kept out of the decisionmaking process, he said, the strategies used by the foreign agencies involved in the operations probably undermined the communities they served, leaving them even more dependent. The operational machinery his agency had brought in during the emergency would have to be passed on to another foreign agency to manage. For instance, local communities could not maintain their water supplies, which would therefore have to be handed over to other agencies to maintain. And even in the more direct area of food aid, passing control of food security on to the local population also created problems. In short, relief operations, very much an external activity focused on saving lives, had set in motion a range of technologies that the local communities were ill equipped to operate and maintain.

One Sudanese scholar went to the extreme of arguing that, all things considered, it would have been better to leave the people to deal with their plight in their own way, even if they starved. "There was an alternative to relief aid," he said. "Let people be hungry; they will eventually find ways of producing food. . . . Yes, we should have been left alone. . . . This is the position I have finally come to. It is the only way out of this chronic dependency. It would have been better had the people died, because people had been dying anyway in different forms."

A member of the affected rural communities almost certainly would not have used such harsh language against food aid. The words of the scholar indicate the deep division between the rural victims of famine and the elite at the center, whose national pride is cushioned by food security.

Relationship among Relief, Recovery, and Development

Whatever the cost in other terms, intervention did indeed perform the critical function of saving lives. The question is whether this objective could have been achieved in harmony with other social, cultural, and economic considerations and whether the infrastructure resulting from relief operations could have been directed toward the mid- to long-term objectives of rehabilitation and development.

Some respondents were quite positive about the link between the infrastructure established in the relief operations and the subsequent phases of rehabilitation and development. They generally felt that the relief agencies concerned should be responsible for establishing the link and for the mutual reinforcement. The agencies, they felt, should use the infrastructure, the contact, the personal involvement with the community, and the overall experience with the emergency to see how what had been established and the lessons learned could be applied to the continuing challenges of relief, rehabilitation, and development. The importance of doing so is accentuated by the likelihood that droughts and the threat of famine will recur. The capacity of the country and the people to meet these emergencies must be enhanced and integrated into the development process.

Particular attention should be given to programs that address the problems of drought-prone areas specifically. Among the measures suggested were establishing storage facilities and generating coop-

erative interest at the village level so that communities can help themselves attack the problems of productivity. Such activities in one
community could have ripple effects in other communities. Once
villagers saw people in neighboring villages "pulling themselves up
by their own bootstraps," they would be likely to emulate them. That
kind of modest but effective process of change could generate and
sustain development from within in a way that emergency relief aid
from outside cannot achieve in any lasting way.

Such an approach was also recommended by the companion OEOA
evaluation in Ethiopia, which placed great emphasis on enhancing
food security at the village level. The study concluded that "a policy
of real incentives to Ethiopian peasant farmers—together with, of
course, other support of a material and social nature—is indispens-
able, if the Ethiopian nation is to emancipate itself from its position
as one of the poorest in the world, one which is dependent on foreign
compassion and the caprices of mass media."[15]

The issue of linking relief operations with the recovery and the mid-
to long-term development of Africa was comprehensively covered by
the report of the UN Working Group on the Linkages between Emergency Relief and Development.[16] The report identified three main
areas of action in the short term:

(a) rebuilding the physical strength of victims of drought, famine
and conflict, meeting the special recovery needs of dispossessed
and displaced people and refugees, and planning new settle-
ments for them; (b) rehabilitating agricultural, pastoral and other
productive capacities damaged by drought and sustaining improvements in transport and logistical capacities; and (c) mobilizing trade in local and national food surpluses, building food
and seed reserves, and using emergency food aid in ways which
support development.

The report also spelled out in specific terms organizational and
operational measures that need to be taken at various levels to coordinate the mobilization of resources for the recovery and development of sub-Saharan Africa.

The United Nations and other donors have been mindful of the
importance of coordinating projects of recovery and rehabilitation
with relief operations. As Holcombe explained,

The UNDP was also concerned about rehabilitation. One of the initiatives that we took—starting in the latter half of 1984—was to mobilize national expertise and international people available in the Sudan to go out to Darfur and to help the regional government there to prepare a relief and, particularly, a rehabilitation and development strategy of about five years' duration, which was to focus on ways and means to resettle displaced populations in areas that could permit self-reliant agriculture and animal husbandry to take place under the new conditions that existed in the Darfur region.

Most of those involved in allied operations, both Sudanese and expatriate, were eager to gear the emergency operations toward the rehabilitation and development phase. As Gazouli Dafalla, the prime minister of the transitional government, put it,

> I think we are at the stage where we want to do both, relief and rehabilitation, with the stress on rehabilitation and I think at this juncture if aid is not really well targeted it can give rise to a lot of negative side effects. If you go on giving aid to people who don't really need it . . . then these people become like refugees, very much dependent on what you give them, and their drive and their initiative to cater for themselves is going to be hampered. I think all the relief organizations agree that aid ought to be well targeted and ought to be used to help people cater for themselves. That is why an emphasis must be put on food for work. We should employ aid to create projects that are part of rehabilitation so that everybody who is able to work must work to earn his living.

In this respect, the 1984–1986 emergency situation made people more aware of the ability of the rural masses to do things for themselves. This, in turn, meant making effective use of the vital roles of the various participants in their organizational, social, and cultural setting, including the chiefs, elders, young people, and women as operational and functional forces for reconstruction and development. Part of the crisis of development in Africa has been the failure of the governments and their international partners to make effective use of the enormous potential of the human and cultural resource base of traditional society in its proper context. Progress in this area hinges on a change of attitude and a translation of that change of attitude into policies that are more favorable to the rural masses. The international community increasingly recognizes the underlying causes of economic deterioration that have culminated in drought-related famine and the need for a broad-based, culturally sensitive approach to the economic and social development of the rural masses.

Official thinking in the Sudan after Nimeiri's overthrow indicated a decided shift toward giving greater attention to the problems of the rural population. As Dafalla explained in 1986, "I used to say that one paradox of this famine is that the real producer, the small farmer, died of starvation, while the town dwellers, who do not produce what they eat, never died of starvation. They were complaining of high prices, but surviving all the same. . . . Something must be done for the small farmer so that this does not repeat itself."

The next prime minister, Sadiq al-Mahdi, whose political support, as represented by his Ansar followers, was rurally based, also articulated a strong commitment to rural development. His stance was echoed by the minister of finance and national economy and the commissioner for relief and rehabilitation. Their objective was to generate development, especially of food products among the rural populations, with an emphasis on the small holders. Furthermore, there was a broad national, regional, and international consensus on the need for an integrated view sensitive to the ecological balances between the population, the environment, and the productive utilization of resources. Although this remained to be translated into practical reforms and programs, the consensus emerging from emergency operations appeared to have created a climate that had improved the chances for international cooperation focused on development.

While this new climate did not necessarily promise the transfer of massive resources from the rich countries of the North to the undeveloped South, youth movements, private voluntary agencies, and nongovernmental organizations were willing to contribute to the improvement of conditions among the rural poor. Although this momentum is not likely to bring about any radical transformation in the conditions of underdevelopment in those countries, it improves the prospects of generating a broad-based process of development from within, with minimum external inputs. To the extent that such a process will progressively, even if gradually, promote a self-sustaining alleviation of poverty and dire need, its contribution to the long-range objectives of development may prove substantial.

Implicit in these changes of climate was a change from the perception of the rural poor as a helpless, dependent lot, with no creativity or energy to contribute to their own welfare, to a view of them as a dynamic and resourceful population, whose full potential had yet to be realized and utilized. Although the tendency toward dependency in the years 1983–86 was clearly a negative result of food aid, this discovery of rural potential augured well as a basis of self-reliance. It also had a particular appeal to international donors inclined to support and enable low-cost approaches to development.

The emphasis on the rural base growing out of the OEOA experience should not be seen as a surrender on the larger issues of national, regional, and continental development in Africa. Of course, the African challenge of development must be an African responsibility. But the international community recognizes that external inputs are essential, especially given the realities of global interdependence. The real challenge then is to balance domestic and intra-African obligation to make policy with external support.

While the international community demonstrated a surprising eagerness to help with famine relief, it was at the same time unwilling to provide the vast resources required to develop Africa. The evaluations of emergency operations under OEOA in both the Sudan and Ethiopia drew attention to the trend of reduced commitments of resources for nonemergency uses. A senior UN official and an expert in international development cooperation explained the situation this way:

Seeing food aid as the easy way out is also on the side of the donors. They have their food surpluses, they have brownie points. . . . I have not seen—in the response to Africa—any readiness to grapple with the real problems of development in terms of what the industrialized North has to do. There has been a lot of lecturing to Africans about what Africa should do to get the process going, and a lot of it is surely justified: liberating enterprises and making government procedures more effective and so on. One can talk about market incentives to food production and so on; that's the debate. But the corresponding debate about the changes in the economic order, to use an old-fashioned phrase, is quite lacking. Commodity markets—which for most African countries are crucial to their development—that issue was raised ten years ago in UNCTAD [UN Conference on Trade and Development]. Even the financial problems are dealt with essentially as Latin American problems. Whereas in Africa, although the amounts are smaller and the burden is probably greater in terms of capacity to bear that burden. I haven't seen any recognition of that need. Much more is said about how African countries can organize themselves and how there should be more importance attached to food production and so on. That is a point that African governments themselves would recognize. African governments would also advance the concomitant need for changes in the international framework. And that I don't see at all. That's why I tend to be quite pessimistic.

Thus, the people of Africa saw feeding the needy as a globally popular cause demanded of governments—some participants in the Khartoum North-South Round Table Conference defined access to food as a fundamental human right. At the same time, however, resources for helping the poor to develop and thus reducing their vulnerability were not easy to secure. The International Monetary Fund was fighting food subsidies. How can this paradoxical trend be explained, and what option does it offer for the future?

The responses of some of the representatives of the international community on this issue are quite pertinent. Many would of course argue that there is something fundamental and immediate about the need for food that touches the human conscience, especially when it is dramatized by the media. The availability of abundant surpluses in the rich industrialized countries of the world, especially in the West, is also part of the scenario. The picture changes dramatically when the resources required are financial. Indeed, many would argue that the overall generosity of the international community, largely triggered by the media and by the artists who staged relief benefits, cannot be relied upon for the future, even though the involvement of young people in generating support is recognized as a promising development in the world. Live Aid/Band Aid, USA for Africa, and other groups involving young people have recognized that there must be a second stage, and they are insisting that some of the money they raised be used for rehabilitation and development.

In view of the anticipated difficulties in generating funds for development, Africans will increasingly be called upon to fall back on their own resources and resourcefulness. As one UN official put it, "We must be constantly thinking of self-reliance, doing those things that make farmers less dependent on the cash economy rather than more dependent."

A number of people, however, believe that the massive response of the West came as a result of the popular desire to assist poor countries, which had been mounting but could not find causes or outlets. The coincidence of famine at a time when Western granaries were full created a timely humanitarian cause, which triggered the spontaneous response not only of the population but also of relief agencies and especially of nongovernmental organizations that had previously been involved in rural development.

The OEOA information office played an important role in using the press to cultivate this fertile soil of popular response from the West. It fed the media in Europe, the United States, and Canada with information they used most effectively. While most people doubted that both the media interest and the generosity that it was able to tap could be relied upon for the future, there is reason to believe that a momentum for international development cooperation was generated which, if well managed and targeted, can be sustained.

The nature of the response to the emergency clearly signified a reduction of government-to-government bilateral aid in inverse proportion to an increase in contributions by or through the voluntary sector or the nongovernmental organizations. As the West, for example, cut back on its development assistance, nongovernmental organizations seemed to be filling the gap. Whether this will be a sustainable trend remains to be seen. Field workers believed that nongovernmental organizations were potentially more qualified than governments to promote the type of international development cooperation required at the local level, even though the larger the organization, the more likely it is to suffer from the same bureaucratic bottlenecks that affect governments.

Many nongovernmental organizations involved in emergency relief operations had been active earlier in development. Many even saw their relief work as something of a digression from their normal activities, and they were eager to return to development. Since these agencies depend on government or popular support for their activities, the recurrent question was whether the momentum of international assistance generated by the emergency situation and the increasing role of the nongovernmental organizations both in relief operations and in the mid- to long-term development process could be sustained or was merely a passing phase.

Judging from the accounts of representatives of some of the agencies interviewed, the increases in funding indicated that, while official development assistance might be diminishing, donors were responding to the shift toward the dominance of nongovernmental organizations in development cooperation. According to the representative of Save the Children–UK, for instance, the year before the emergency was a year of record income (16.5 million pounds sterling), which rose in the year of the enormous media coverage (42.5 million pounds sterling). The budget of Save the Children–US increased from about $8 million to $65 million. The London-based War on Want, which had expected donations in 1986 to start falling, was pleasantly surprised when they did not. On the other hand, UN sources indicated that their own levels of contribution had begun to slow down in 1985 and that the response had been very poor since 1986 in all nonfood sectors. On balance, the shift toward making funds available to the nongovernmental organizations for relief and development remained rather precarious. The role of the governments would not be eradicated. As one member of the international community noted,

> The problem is that in the final analysis some central body—the central body being the government—has to become more aware that there is an adequate sharing of resources among peoples. That is why we have governments. It would be nice if we could make people-to-people contact: our hands are tied. I see a problem in bypassing governments. Every effort must be made for government commitment.

Moreover, Sudanese and foreign observers shared the perception that too many nongovernmental organizations, both foreign and national, were involved in everyday relief operations and that perhaps in the future the number of such agencies should be restricted. To the extent that this massive involvement signifies a broad-based mobilization of resources for relief, the response should not be to restrict them but to target their resources and energies in a way that can maximize their contribution. The companion Ethiopia report, while viewing nongovernmental organizations as "in many ways the most dynamic and active element of the donor community," anticipated that the government "in due course will perhaps tend to restrict the number of expatriates residing in the country under the auspices of various NGOs."[17]

The role of the United Nations in sustaining the momentum that had been generated by the emergency was generally recognized as critical. UNEOS and the OEOA played a pivotal role in generating and targeting resources for emergency operations in the Sudan. The interaction between the national context and the international community was an essential ingredient in the success of international cooperation, not only with respect to the continuing need for relief but also in the continuing efforts for rehabilitation and development.

Chapter 3

Conflict-Related Famine, 1987–91

Speaking before the United Nations General Assembly on October 7, 1986, Prime Minister Sadiq al-Mahdi thanked the international community for assistance provided to the Sudan. He also conveyed "the good news that the drought in the Sudan is now over and that the country is now able to feed itself from what it produces." Subsequent events demonstrated that his optimism was decidedly premature. Sudanese continued to die because of conflict-related famine in the South, and within a few short years another drought-induced famine would revisit the North. Food shortages are predicted to be even worse in the 1990s than they were in 1984–85.

During the years 1986–88, an estimated 400,000 persons lost their lives. In 1988 alone, deaths resulting from the conflict-related famine in the South reached about 250,000. By 1988, half the population of the southern Sudan had been displaced by the fighting. The year 1989 brought a reprieve, thanks in part to the six-month cessation of fighting associated with Operation Lifeline Sudan. Late in the year, however, the civil war sputtered back to life, setting the stage for more suffering born of conflict and conflict-related food shortages.

OVERVIEW OF OPERATION LIFELINE SUDAN

Operation Lifeline Sudan represented a major international endeavor to deal with the withering ordeal of human suffering in the southern Sudan. With the famine of 1984–86 in the North largely controlled, the scene shifted to the South. Spared the worst of the earlier drought and thus not the scene of OEOA-associated relief efforts, the South was particularly hard hit by drought in 1986–88.

The policies of the warring parties, the government of the Sudan and the insurgent Sudan People's Liberation Army (SPLA), compounded the problems associated with poor harvests from failing rains over large areas of the South. Fighting a war that grew out of political, religious, racial, ethnic, and economic differences, the antagonists adopted military policies that directly and indirectly, by default and by design, created famine and other hardships. They successfully disrupted normal agricultural and economic patterns, forcing people to seek refuge in towns and remoter areas in the South and in rural and urban areas in the North, particularly around Khartoum.

The government equipped tribal militias with sophisticated weapons that they used against populations suspected of loyalty to the SPLA. The insurgents encircled towns representing the remaining outposts of government authority and presence in the South. Both sides interfered with relief supplies bound for areas controlled by their opponents, suspecting that they contained military items or that the supplies would confer military advantage. In 1986, 1987, and 1988, the SPLA threatened civilian planes and actually downed several, including a relief aircraft. The insurgents attacked convoys carrying relief supplies over land and by river. The Khartoum authorities also impeded relief efforts, strictly limiting relief activities and expelling four relief groups altogether.[1]

International frustrations in responding to massive suffering and intensive diplomatic activities resulted in a conference on relief operations held under UN auspices in March 1989 in Khartoum that launched Operation Lifeline Sudan. Central to the initiative was recognition of the principle that all civilians have a right to humanitarian assistance, wherever they are located. To facilitate that access, the government and later the insurgents agreed to arrangements that established certain "corridors of tranquility" through which relief would safely pass. This agreement set the stage for what UN officials described as one of history's largest humanitarian interventions in an active civil war.

The Khartoum conference and the activities it spurred galvanized the international community. During 1989 resources of some $205 million were channeled directly to Lifeline. As much as another $100 million was mobilized for Sudanese relief in general. Lifeline also played major roles in transporting and distributing the relief supplies themselves, although a system for doing so took longer to set up than expected. By the end of 1989, however, Lifeline had exceeded its 107,000-ton target of food aid and had also provided 3,760 tons of important nonfood inputs, including agricultural hand tools, seeds, human and animal vaccines and medicines, and shelter materials. Food and livestock production rebounded, and nutrition showed measurable improvement.

The intangible contributions of Lifeline were perhaps more important than its direct benefits. The presence of international aid personnel contributed to a sense of well-being among the people throughout the South and moderated the worst excesses of the warring parties. The advent of outside food assistance broke the merchants' corner on the market, putting food prices more nearly within the reach of all. Perhaps most important, the agreement creating corridors of tranquility was extended month by month from April into October, when the war broke out once again. The absence of hostilities did far more than allow relief vehicles, supplies, and personnel to accomplish their work. It encouraged a more general return to the normal agricultural and economic pursuits disrupted by the fighting.

Lifeline also survived a transition of governments. Prime Minister Sadiq al-Mahdi was overthrown in a military coup in late June 1989. The new chief of state, Brigadier General Omar Hassan Ahmed al-Bashir, at once reaffirmed the commitment of the new regime to Lifeline, but the Muslim fundamentalist government he headed eventually took a much tougher line toward relief activities.

Lifeline II got under way in March 1990 when, after considerable delay, the warring parties reaffirmed their commitment to the humanitarian principles and operational arrangements of the earlier agreement. At that time, the United Nations appealed for 100,000 metric tons of food, roughly comparable to the target of the original Lifeline. Between April and December 1990, almost all of that amount was delivered despite major logistical obstacles.

In the interest of spurring reconstruction, Lifeline operations in 1990 placed even heavier emphasis than during the previous year on nonfood inputs. Less bulky commodities made for a corresponding reduction in transportation costs. There were also other positive developments. The UN International Children's Emergency Fund reported that the vaccines Lifeline had made available and the cold-chain networks it had established had provided immunization coverage of an estimated 66 percent in government-controlled areas and as high as 70 percent in portions of SPLA territory.

The difficulties Lifeline had experienced in late 1989 continued and intensified in 1990. Each side accused the United Nations of partiality toward the other. The government, alleging that Lifeline had violated Sudanese sovereignty by providing cover for military support for the insurgents, demanded tighter operational controls and accountability. The SPLA, which claimed more of the South than it had at the beginning of Lifeline I, sought a larger proportion of the available relief supplies while resisting calls for increased accountability.

In view of the difficulties relief operations had routinely encountered, some argued it would be wrong to extend Lifeline. Doing so would leave unchallenged the indignities it was suffering. Others held that a new agreement could reenergize commitments of the warring parties, overcome practical difficulties, and rekindle international support. They also believed that the presence of international relief personnel throughout the South would allow for continued monitoring of civilian needs and military activities and for rapid resumption of emergency assistance if and when needed. While Lifeline activities were indeed extended, the program failed to get the antagonists to cooperate more fully with each other.

In reviewing the situation at the July 1991 session of the UN Economic and Social Council in Geneva, Per Janvid, the secretary-general's special coordinator for emergency and relief operations in the Sudan, recalled the historical importance of Lifeline. "A historical precedent had been established in 1989," he said, "when the Government of Sudan and the Sudanese People's Liberation Movement agreed that the delivery of humanitarian assistance to war affected civilians, wherever they might be, should transcend both military and political considerations." He observed, "This enlightened and practical approach to meeting humanitarian needs in time of war has been widely acclaimed by the international community, and continues to be recognized by many as a model for humanitarian assistance in other countries contending with 'complex emergencies.'"

The bulk of Janvid's report, however, was more negative. "While one can praise the principles of Operation Lifeline Sudan," he observed, "one cannot ignore the difficulties of putting them into practice." He went on to note that while "substantial quantities of food assistance were initially intended to have been transported by UN train and barge convoys through conflict areas, . . . despite protracted negotiations neither train nor barge in the course of 1990 ever left on its humanitarian mission. Similarly, no road corridor through conflict zones had ever been opened during the year; hence, certain areas designated for relief food were never reached."[2] All in all, some 93 percent of the food aid needed in the latter part of 1990 was transported.

The pall that had settled over Lifeline by the beginning of 1991 continued through the time of Janvid's report in July. Despite some positive changes in attitudes, fundamental problems persisted. The government had announced in May that difficulties had been resolved and Lifeline III had been launched, but the parties involved had not agreed on an operational plan. The United Nations and donors, rejecting talk of Lifeline III, saw Lifeline II continuing as an "interim arrangement," which suggests their own ambivalence about its future.

A report by an AID assessment team, based on six weeks' experience in the southern Sudan in April and May 1991, provided additional details regarding the situation on the ground. The team concluded that the months until the next harvest in September–October "will undoubtedly be a period of hardship." However, the group expressed the view that "mass starvation will not occur" in the three dozen towns and villages it had visited.

At the same time, the team found the umbrella provided by Lifeline "inadequate to respond to all critical needs in southern Sudan." Under the terms of the Lifeline agreement, movements of trucks, aircraft, and barges transporting relief supplies required both government and SPLA consent. The insurgents had provided blanket approval, while the Khartoum authorities had "variously withheld approval entirely, provided approval for limited locations, or provided approval for as little as one week." The report's detailed chronology of the difficulties illustrates problems that, with the exception of the period from April to September 1989, had beset relief efforts to one degree or another throughout 1986–91 and into 1992:

No barge movements have ever been approved by the GOS [Government of the Sudan], effectively precluding the delivery of any appreciable supply of commodities to Ler and Yirol under the OLS [Operation Lifeline Sudan] umbrella. Truck convoys were similarly disallowed from the end of November 1990 until March 18, 1991—limiting deliveries by road to a one-month period, mid-March to mid-April. At the end of September 1990, the GOS cut the list of sites accessible by air from 18 to eight, a condition that prevailed until the end of the year, at which time the GOS banned relief flights entirely for a period of three weeks. Flights to eight locations were allowed from January 22 to February 22, but were again banned from February 23 to March 7. The GOS permitted flights to four locations from March 8 to 15, but then again halted all flights, this time until April 30. From April 30 until about May 10, the GOS allowed flights to five locations and, since then has granted permission for OLS flights to 11 locations. However, by the time the UN was able to make the necessary preparations to fly to one of these (Akon), the GOS withdrew permission for unspecified "security reasons."[3]

Although interference by the insurgents with relief activities at the time of the team's visit was not as blatant as interference by the government, the SPLA had earlier created substantial obstacles. Moreover, the AID team singled out for criticism several practices of the insurgents. It noted, for example, that the Sudan Relief and Rehabilitation Association (SRRA) lacked a systematic approach to the allocation of available international relief supplies based on need. It also questioned the distribution of food aid at a camp for displaced persons, where some of the inhabitants, including young boys, were in training for the armed insurgent forces.

Such difficulties in 1991 were of a piece with those experienced in 1990 and in late 1989, although program managers noted that the tonnages transported in 1991 reached a new high. Difficulties continued to plague the program in 1992 as well. On each occasion the process of obtaining agreement of the warring parties brought certain short-term benefits, even though none of the arrangements proved to be durable. One of the frustrations Lifeline encountered was the sense of futility relief workers experienced in regularly reaffirming basic humanitarian principles that the parties to the conflict then ignored. After more than three years of massive international assistance, cooperation with Lifeline remained tenuous, and the integrity of aid activities required daily protection.

Continuing difficulties in the South notwithstanding, international attention, which had shifted from the northern Sudan in 1983–86 to the southern Sudan in 1987–90, looked more to the North once again by late 1990. Assessments by the UN Food and Agriculture Organization (FAO) and the World Food Program (WFP) concluded that the drought was worse in scale than that of 1984–85 and that the floundering national economy and resurgent civil war were even more formidable obstacles to an effective relief program. Meanwhile, a report by the AID Famine Early Warning System predicted a food deficit that would require "ten times the amount of aid needed during the 1984–85 famine which claimed the lives of more than 250,000 victims."[4]

On March 14, 1991, the UN secretary-general made a "consolidated appeal" for a staggering $716,583,400, covering the food and nonfood needs of emergency operations in the North and of continuing relief operations in the South. "Consolidated" were the resources needed for both North and South, with Janvid functioning as special coordinator for both areas. The Sudan's humanitarian crisis had come full circle. Drought-induced famine reminiscent of 1983–86 had returned to the North. The conflict-related famine to which Lifeline responded in 1989 continued in the South. Each of the four major problem areas that had complicated relief operations in the earlier years was intensified by civil strife.

INTERVENING FROM OUTSIDE

Internecine conflict within the Sudan exacerbated the normal difficulties of adapting international relief to the particulars of a given local situation. By underscoring the foreign aspects of relief, the conflict made assistance more suspect, complicating its chances of success.

Human needs and attempts to meet them came to be viewed from a political-military vantage point. What were the presumed allegiances and strategic importance of the civilian population at risk, and how would assistance to reduce their vulnerability affect the outcome of the war? "When you're at war," observed John Beavan, Britain's ambassador to the Sudan in 1990, "everything becomes a question of military and strategic advantage."[5] Relief operations are likely to be agreed to only when perceived as benefiting one's own side, or at least as avoiding disproportionate advantage to one's adversary, and are likely to be curtailed or discontinued otherwise.

The government of the Sudan and the SPLA each agreed to participate in Lifeline only when their respective interests seemed to be clearly served by doing so. In early 1989, the military situation was such that each side needed a reprieve—the government to recoup from a string of battlefield losses, the insurgents to consolidate recent military successes. Politically, too, the time was propitious. The government of Sadiq al-Mahdi was weak and under pressure to end the war; the insurgents could use time to establish their authority in areas newly under their control. Both welcomed the chance to reinstate themselves in the good graces of the international community.

Even granted the benefits each warring side would receive from participating in Lifeline, each suspected that food would be appropriated by the other side and feared that relief shipments contained weapons and other items to strengthen the opposing military. The government had a special concern: that entering into an agreement on relief would confer legitimacy on the insurgency, which it had taken pains never to recognize. In short, each side sought to use Lifeline for its own advantage while accusing the other side of doing so as well. Each needed assurances that relief would be scrupulously impartial and carefully monitored to prevent abuses.

The principles and operational arrangements of Lifeline provided such assurances. In consenting to them, the government made clear that it was doing so as an exercise of its sovereign authority. "We have, in effect, conceded sovereignty over a large part of our territory to the United Nations," commented Ohag Mohamed Musa, minister of social welfare. In return, he noted, "We expect close monitoring by the United Nations."[6] The insurgents, the de facto government in most of the South, exercised the equivalent of sovereign rights in agreeing to Lifeline and also kept a watchful eye on relief operations.

During the middle six months of 1989, when the political-military needs of both parties to the conflict made for cooperation with Lifeline, relief operations proceeded reasonably well, although relief officials on a daily basis had to assert themselves to protect their activities. Late in 1989, however, when the political-military situation changed and the war resumed in earnest, cooperation with Lifeline no longer suited the immediate interests of either side. As each of the warring parties reclaimed its sovereignty and narrowed the geographical and political space open to humanitarian activities, the effectiveness of relief efforts suffered.

A normal antidote to suspicion is transparency. The International Committee of the Red Cross (ICRC), whose assistance to people in civil war settings continually generates suspicion among belligerents, emphasizes the need for impartiality and neutrality. In 1988, when famine deaths reached an all-time high, the ICRC labored from March until December before winning the agreement of both sides to allow relief flights to an equal number of locations on both sides. First one party and then the other objected. Almost two years later, activities were still the object of suspicion, despite the fact that the ICRC filed flight plans with both sides and reported in detail on its activities to ensure transparency.

When the Sudan government suspended relief flights, it did not admit, of course, that it was doing so because the aid activities no longer suited its purposes. It repeated its suspicions so often they took on a reality of their own, which even the most transparent behavior was unable to overcome. Government suspicions were fueled by the actions of some nongovernmental organizations, which, placing a higher premium on responding to human need than on respecting sovereignty, had flown relief supplies into the South without government permission. Clearly the process of building and rebuilding trust is far more difficult during a civil war than when a natural disaster has caused an emergency.

A second area in which war heightened the difficulty of harmonizing a foreign intervention with local sensitivities concerned the general perception that Lifeline represented a judgment on the Sudan government and a threat to its way of life. The fact that aid was necessitated because of the demonstrable failure of Sudanese institutions underscored a widespread sense of guilt. Since famine is preventable, writes Alex de Waal, its existence represents "an indictment of the ethics of the society in which it has occurred."[7]

The extent to which international relief was a source of embarrassment is reflected in comments made in 1986 by Prime Minister Gazouli Dafalla. "It is painful for us to accept these gifts you bear us," he observed. "It is painful to listen to your admonitions as to the manner in which we are using what you are giving us. The Sudanese way is to bestow gifts upon the people who come to this country, not the other way around. While you are doing a noble thing, it is hurting us. Every grain [of food], in effect, is hurting the Sudanese. It is painful to receive it for nothing." Interviewed four years later during the Lifeline study, he expressed similar sentiments, if anything even more charged with resentment.

The Sudanese sense of being embarrassed and overwhelmed that was associated with the OEOA initiative was heightened by Lifeline. The massive infusion of outside resources and personnel came at a time when the very identity of the Sudan was being fought out on the battlefield. Precisely when the Sudan's traditions were most sorely tested, external assistance appeared to confirm their inadequacy and contribute to their erosion.

Religion, both as a factor in the civil war and as an element implicit in the relief initiative, underscored the external nature of the intervention. The civil war was not, first and foremost, about religion. Religious differences were only one of many factors in the conflict—by some accounts—not the most deep-seated, even though the politicization of religion and society has now brought the issue to the forefront of the conflict.

Since Nimeiri's introduction of the *shari'a* (Islamic laws), upheld by successive governments and consolidated by the fundamentalist regime that came to power in mid-1989, religion has indeed become the most divisive factor in the conflict. While the current regime has acknowledged no separation between religion and the state, the SPLA is a secular movement committed to freedom of religious expression within a single Sudan. Thus, even though many diverse disagreements fuel the war, "the religious dimension [became] symbolic of all that is contested."[8]

The religious element in the conflict drew attention to the Western nature of Lifeline and, in particular, to the religious aspects of the relief intervention. While expressing gratitude for the aid received, the Khartoum authorities were acutely conscious of its origins in the Christian West and of its delivery by a host of Christian nongovernmental organizations, some committed to spreading their religious faith as well as to saving lives.

The mere fact that Christians were involved, even motivated by common humanitarian ideals, became provocative to some Muslims. In certain quarters Lifeline was portrayed as a violation of the beliefs and integrity of a Muslim nation. The clash of religions in the civil war thus made for heightened perceptions of the external nature of the relief effort. While in the popular mind UN and government aid was not beyond suspicion, aid channeled through private and, in many cases, religious organizations was particularly suspect.

It was probably no coincidence that the four nongovernmental organizations that the government expelled from the Sudan in 1987 all had Christian ties: the Lutheran World Federation, World Vision International, Association of Christian Resource Organizations Serving Sudan (ACROSS), and the Swedish Free Mission. Nor was it surprising that the government worked closely with Muslim aid institutions (which made those same institutions suspect to international donors) or that the SPLA cultivated the New Sudan Council of Churches, a wartime offshoot of the Khartoum-based Sudan Council of Churches, which had experienced difficulty carrying out programs in SPLA-controlled areas during the war.

Islam, traditional tribal religions, and Christianity as practiced in the Sudan each had certain humanitarian features. Muslims had a well-established private and public system of mutual support and reciprocity. Black Southerners, Christian and otherwise, also had built-in traditions of assisting the needy. Tribal chiefs had an obligation to assist the destitute, even from outside their own areas; emergency needs were viewed not as a moral stigma but as a sign of hard times caused by factors beyond an individual's control.

The religious tensions fanned by the war, however, undermined traditional commitments to humane values. For some Muslims, the bitterness and length of conflict-related famine eroded Islamic obligations of generosity. For some Christians and practitioners of traditional religions, the threatened use of governmental structures to enforce fundamentalist Islamic principles eroded good will toward Muslims.

The Sudanese tradition of neighborliness was also seriously compromised by the war. The Sudanese have always prided themselves on their hospitality to other Sudanese, to refugees from neighboring lands, and to expatriates from overseas. The sheer scale of human displacement represented by the civil war and by similar upheavals elsewhere in the region, however, overwhelmed the country's ability to provide the accustomed food, shelter, and welcome.

"At any one time over the past three years," the secretary general's special coordinator noted in his 1991 report to the UN Economic and Social Council, about 20 percent of the nation's population has had "to move from their homes in search of food, employment, and security. For the people of Sudan, this sad fact poses a dilemma. With a long and deep rooted tradition of hospitality, town dwellers and those in rural areas nevertheless are often faced with large numbers of displaced people that have no choice but to drain available resources and strain local infrastructures."[9]

The large refugee population to which the Sudan also played host and provided assistance complicated the unsettling effects of massive internal displacement. By 1991, some 800,000 persons had sought refuge in the Sudan from countries such as Chad, Uganda, Zaire, and Ethiopia. Only about half of these were receiving international assistance through UN agencies.

The overthrow of the Mengistu government, which had supported the SPLA in its war against the Sudan government, unleashed a flow of some 50,000 refugees from Ethiopia. Many of these refugees were former Ethiopian government soldiers seeking asylum and protection in the northern Sudan. At the same time, several hundred thousand Sudanese refugees who had resided in camps in Ethiopia that were managed by the SPLA returned to the South in anticipation of friction with the new regime in Ethiopia.

In their appeals to the international community for assistance, Sudanese authorities affirmed the Sudan's traditions of hospitality. In a statement issued in June 1991, Colonel Mohammed al-Amin Khalifa, member of the Revolutionary Command Council, noted that the government had mobilized all possible resources, "based on its commitments to brotherhood, neighborliness rights and the charters of the United Nations and the [Organization of African Unity] and our religious doctrines and causes of humanity, which oblige us to extend help to others in need and to share our food with the refugees." Since the government's own resources were clearly unequal to the task, however, Khalifa called on "the international community to pay due attention to this humanitarian issue before it becomes a tragedy."[10]

The sheer scale of the Lifeline operation upstaged what the Sudan itself was providing, rankling the authorities in Khartoum. It also overshadowed, Sudanese officials believed, their own contribution in agreeing in the middle of a civil war to participate in Lifeline in the first place. The government viewed the exchange rate it granted Lifeline as an annual contribution of some 90 million Sudanese pounds. It complained bitterly that relief workers and human rights groups continued attacks against Sudanese life and institutions instead of giving the government credit for extending the effectiveness of the program. Even when Lifeline became the basis for similar initiatives elsewhere in Africa, the expected recognition was not forthcoming.

There were also frictions at a more operational level. Aid activities thrust people of different backgrounds, orientations, and values together in circumstances that demand cooperation yet amplify differences. Many of the relief workers were new to the Sudan and had no prior background in Arabic language and culture. The absence of greater cross-cultural awareness and understanding significantly undercut the effectiveness of the common effort.

To its credit, Lifeline sought to minimize the external nature of the relief intervention by strengthening Sudanese institutions. It worked to enhance the capacity of the Relief and Resettlement Commission (RRC) on the government side and the Sudan Relief and Rehabilitation Association (SRRA) on the insurgents' side. Founded during the earlier emergency to facilitate international relief matters, the RRC received staff members and other support from Lifeline. The SRRA, which started from scratch in early 1989, received funds, vehicles, management training, and other support from UNICEF, governments, and nongovernmental organizations.

The results of such strengthening efforts were uneven at best. They were more successful with the SRRA than with the RRC. "Our emphasis in Lifeline," explained Lifeline's Nairobi-based southern sector coordinator, "has been to ensure that at the end of the operation, we would have built and left in place a capacity among the population and our counterparts to sustain programs of rehabilitation."[11] After two years of such interaction, the SRRA had begun to play a more assertive and constructive role, although cooperation remained far from steady. Developments in late 1991 and early 1992 indicated considerable slippage in this regard.

Some strengthening of indigenous NGOs also took place. Here, too, however, efforts were uneven, with the favoritism for expatriate NGOs noted during OEOA days putting qualified Sudanese private organizations at a disadvantage. The sense of exclusion from Lifeline activities expressed by a number of Sudanese NGOs and government officials had a basis in reality. International relief managers placed a higher premium on getting the emergency job done than on collaborating with Sudanese counterparts. In addition to the operational benefits that might have accrued from the deliberate mobilization of indigenous groups, Lifeline missed an opportunity to minimize the alien nature of its assistance. In retrospect, Sudanese institutions, private and public alike, probably could have been strengthened without unduly retarding the pace of relief activities.

The management of information about Lifeline by UN officials occasioned similar criticisms and had similar effects. Because they viewed Western media as their gateway to European and North American publics and resources, UN officials did not give high priority to cultivating Sudanese, Kenyan, and other Arab and African media. Lifeline thus lost an opportunity to create a non-Western constituency and fueled suspicion of its operations as a foreign intervention driven by Western political interests. Efforts made to enlist Arab governments in relief activities also did not bear fruit.

The war itself was a reason that Sudanese institutions did not share more equitably in relief activities. Well into Lifeline, both the RRC and the SRRA still lacked the degree of independence from the political authorities, even in humanitarian matters, that donors hoped for. Their lack of independence exacerbated normal concerns about the abuse of relief supplies.

"Given the risk of the political and/or military manipulation of relief assistance," notes Gayle Smith, a knowledgeable observer of the Horn of Africa, "donors are inclined to play a more dominant role and to scrutinize aspects of a relief operation that might, in peacetime, go unmonitored. The consequence is often that little or no effort is made to increase local capacity to manage disasters." Unless such local capacity is strengthened, she concludes, "a dangerous dependency will set in and the need for external intervention will increase rather than decrease."[12]

In the Sudan there were particular frustrations in early 1990 when Lifeline II was trying to get under way, in early 1991 when attempts to persuade Khartoum to request assistance for the North were thwarted, and in both years when the government refused aid institutions a favorable exchange rate. At these times aid workers were heard to assert that "we" care about the Sudanese people more than the Sudanese political authorities do themselves. Relief efforts did not become a vehicle for overcoming the separation of the outside "we" and the inside "they" by seeking out and reinforcing points of caring within the Sudan itself.

In fact, relief operations themselves represented a setback to such solidarity. To hear the Sudanese tell it, white outsiders dominated relief activities. Many of these foreigners had no previous professional contact with the Sudan or Africa and no long-term commitment to the Sudan's people and their future. UN officials counter that they did give priority to employing Africans, with expatriates brought in only for jobs that could not be filled locally. Both points of view contain some truth. The negative message conveyed by very junior expatriates may have exceeded their actual numbers, but UN staffing decisions invited such reactions.

Negative perceptions of aid intervention were not, of course, unique to Lifeline. Aid activities in the Sudan earlier in the decade had stirred up similar resistance. OEOA activities in Ethiopia in 1984–86 also suffered from "strained" relations between expatriate aid workers and nationals, reflecting "a sense of wounded national pride and unde-sired independence on the Ethiopian side, and unwitting arrogance among foreigners." The companion OEOA study of Ethiopia also chided donor governments for insisting that their aid contributions be used to hire their own nationals.[13]

The war situation guaranteed that the intrusive aspect of interna-tional assistance would be an irritant and an unavoidable object of suspicion. Yet relief operations failed to do everything they might have to ease the existing sense of guilt and assaulted sensibilities or to minimize their intrinsic foreignness by collaborating effectively with local institutions. Indeed, their failure to do so underscored their alien nature.

FRAMING THE CONTEXT

In cases of natural disaster such as the drought-induced famine of 1983–86, relief operations need to be mounted with careful attention to their economic, social, and political context. Famines of this sort should be understood in relation to such underlying matters as ag-ricultural and land-use policies, population pressures, settlement pat-terns, and environmental conservation.

Civil strife intensifies both the difficulty and the necessity of making the connections between relief activities and contextual realities. The superficial reason is clear: two different sets of political authorities must be accommodated. At a deeper level, their struggle has a direct bearing on the ability of aid efforts to contribute to progress on critical issues of peace, human rights, and development.

During its heyday in 1989, Lifeline made a positive link with such contextual concerns. For example, Lifeline helped establish a climate in which hostilities were attenuated.[14] The corridors of tranquility, originally negotiated to ensure safe passage for relief supplies, had broader and somewhat serendipitous results. Closed to military vehicles but open to relief convoys, the corridors encouraged the return of normal commerce, greatly benefiting the surrounding countryside. The cease-fires and truces declared by the warring parties within the corridors reduced military activity over far wider areas. The narrow corridors of tranquility became, in effect, broader zones of peace.

However problematic their external nature, international relief operations served as a point of agreement between the warring parties at a time when there were few such common bonds. On several occasions, agreement on Lifeline helped keep alive the floundering peace negotiations. One session was about to break up when a government official in desperation proposed that both sides reaffirm their commitment to ensure relief to all in need. After all, he said, those who are suffering are "not strangers but our own children." Moved by the appeal, SPLA officials reaffirmed their own commitment to the children of the Sudan.[15]

The importance of such common ground should not be underestimated. Abdalla A. Abdalla, the Sudan's ambassador to the United States, explained in early 1990 that the critical issue for the warring parties was not the need for external pressure to "bring them to the realization that the war has been very destructive." Since they both were fully aware of the suffering generated by the war, the missing link was "how to find common grounds for peace."[16]

In addition to providing such common grounds, Lifeline itself benefited from the peace stirrings that were gaining in strength at the time. In late 1988 and early 1989, a growing Sudanese constituency for peace, comprising several northern political parties, trade unions, and academic, human rights, professional, and religious groups, was pressing the government of Prime Minister Sadiq al-Mahdi for a negotiated settlement to the war. Participation in Lifeline offered both the government and the SPLA a way to demonstrate their sincerity about alleviating suffering and dealing with its underlying causes.

These substantial contributions notwithstanding, Lifeline did little to address or to resolve the conflict itself. Why did the international community fail to extend the collaboration between the warring parties achieved on relief into something more durable? The conflict did not lend itself to easy resolution. After about six months of relative tranquility, which had provided protected space for relief work, the war was rekindled. Humanitarian need had not been a controlling factor in the decision of either party to participate in Lifeline in the first place, and Lifeline likewise did not deter a resumption of hostilities. Moreover, the advent of a harder-line regime in Khartoum—which Lifeline could not have prevented but may indeed have helped provoke—did not enhance the prospects either of peace or of cooperative relief efforts.

One factor contributing to the missed opportunity was that the United Nations was not organized to proceed on both the relief front and the peace front in tandem. It viewed the task of avoiding famine deaths through Lifeline as self-contained, unrelated to the task of ending the war. "There was nothing in my mandate at all empowering me to negotiate an end to the conflict," recalled James P. Grant, the secretary-general's personal representative. Such an effort would require a formal invitation from the Sudan government to the secretary-general, said Grant and UN senior officials in New York, and such an invitation was never offered.[17]

The missed opportunity is all the more lamentable because the parties to the conflict themselves expressed regret that Lifeline failed to help draw the war to an end. This suggests that more creativity in developing a peace initiative might have borne fruit. Noting that "one of the major factors that motivates the continuation of the war is the lack of confidence and trust between the warring parties," President Bashir observed that "an operation like Lifeline—a situation in which you have relief moving across battle lines—might help by building a foundation of trust between the protagonists."[18] Ambassador Abdalla, too, lamented that Lifeline had not continued the process of cooperation, moving beyond corridors of tranquility and cease-fires to tackle the outstanding political differences. While such utterances may seem like crocodile tears, they may also reflect genuine disappointment.

Complicating the picture still further is evidence that relief operations themselves were in certain respects implicated in the continuation of the strife. While the direct appropriation of relief supplies by the troops on each side seems not to have been a major problem—at least in the first six months of Lifeline—there were many less obvious interconnections between relief and the conflict.

The availability of relief food probably consolidated the hold of the warring parties over their respective populations by alleviating the conditions of civilians on both sides. Certainly it eased the belligerents' own need to provide such food—or to foster conditions in which food could be produced locally. The warring parties also used the tranquility associated with Lifeline to prepare for renewed combat. Such unwelcome effects qualify the positive role the relief operation played in moderating the conduct of the war. Moreover, the difficulties encountered by Lifeline I after the civil war had resumed confirm the view that continued relief, however necessary, remains at best a palliative if it does not address the conflict itself. After all, "the reason we're in need of help in this conflict," observed Gazouli Dafalla, "*is* this conflict."[19]

Given the complexity of the causes of the war, a serious concern for peace would necessarily have required as major a commitment as the relief activities themselves. Such an effort would have needed to be initiated early, receive high-level political encouragement, and command substantial diplomatic and financial resources. In the absence of such a strategy, relief itself would have continued to dominate the scene. Indeed, relief operations have a way of becoming an all-consuming preoccupation.

Lifeline had positive effects in the related areas of human rights and development, even though once again the absence of a strategy based on sensitivity to the local context meant that the broader potential of the relief program was not realized. Here, too, the complicating role played by the conflict is evident.

Much of the improvement in the human rights situation after 1988 came as a result of the activities and presence of personnel associated with Lifeline. Reporting on the loss of some 250,000 lives through famine and war in that grim year when relief efforts were largely blocked, the U.S. State Department noted that "until late in the year, elements of the competing forces frequently interfered or failed to cooperate with international relief efforts in order to gain advantage in the civil war. As a result of such interference, and of government negligence or inefficiency, many displaced persons suffered from severe malnutrition, and there were many deaths due to starvation and disease."[20]

A year later, Amnesty International credited "cease-fires declared by the government and the SPLA, combined with a massive United Nations effort to get food into famine affected areas in the south," with contributing to a significant reduction in human rights violations. Unfortunately, the return of violence late in the year and the recurring difficulties of relief personnel in securing access to the civilian population were reflected in a subsequent upswing in abuses of human rights.[21]

Relief activities also had a positive effect on development. While food was the largest single relief input transported in 1989, Lifeline from the start also provided significant amounts of nonfood items such as seeds and tools geared to the rehabilitation of agriculture. An even greater emphasis on medium- to longer-term economic and social change characterized the planning of Lifeline activities in 1990–91, however frustrated in their implementation.

Relief personnel, particularly through cross-border activities mounted from Kenya into SPLA areas, provided technical assistance in the health and education sectors from the beginning of the program. The SRRA, whose work was actively supported by aid agencies, took its rehabilitation mandate seriously, with staff members assigned to such sectors as agriculture, health, education, and employment.

Periodic assessments of needs, carried out by the SRRA, the United Nations, and nongovernmental organizations, also stressed post-emergency inputs. The primary purpose of the AID mission in early 1991, described earlier, was to forecast the extent of malnutrition and famine later in the year. It recommended accelerated delivery of seeds and fishing equipment, development of alternative crops and fishing cooperatives, and rehabilitation of health facilities and services.

One of the key differences in Lifeline's effect in insurgent-controlled and government-controlled areas was precisely in the area of development. The government lost control of some of the rural areas and towns to the SPLA, leaving the three provincial capitals of Juba, Malakal, and Wau as its major footholds in the South. Encircled and occasionally shelled by the insurgents, these cities were badly in need of food and medicine and had limited opportunities for agricultural production and other self-help development activities.

Moreover, at a time when those Lifeline programs managed from

Khartoum were constrained by the authorities, many similar activities under way in SPLA-controlled areas proceeded on their own. To be sure, vaccination programs relying on air transportation for their shipments of serum were affected by the government's ban on relief flights. However, activities for which ground transportation sufficed—some of them directed by Sudanese nationals for whom entry into the South was not a problem—carried on apace. At meetings between Lifeline authorities and representatives of the warring parties, government officials were sometimes dismayed to discover the extent and scope of the reconstruction activities taking place in SPLA-controlled areas.

Contributing to the differences between the scope of activities in each area was the frustration felt by the international community toward the authorities in Khartoum. Their interference with relief activities led many governments to refuse to provide aid except for emergency purposes. Canadian nongovernmental organizations, feeling that aid allowed the Sudanese government "to use other funds for the perpetuation of the war effort and the costs of suppressing its own population," urged Ottawa to withdraw all government-to-government assistance, directing funds for humanitarian and development work instead only through private channels. When Lifeline was launched, the Canadian government itself had articulated a similar concern. "In the absence of a peace settlement and national reconciliation," its delegate to the Khartoum conference in early 1989 had stated, "we will consider seriously whether continuing assistance of other than a purely humanitarian nature can be justified."[22]

The success of such efforts at rehabilitation and development was inhibited by the threat of war and, on occasion, by the war itself. The return of normalcy to the Torit area, largely a function of intensive relief efforts, received a serious setback when a government bombing mission in June 1990 disrupted poultry-raising and educational activities. Even though much of the South had not seen actual conflict for some time, the possibility that hostilities might be rekindled lent a tentative character to postemergency efforts.

Beyond the positive and negative effects of emergency operations on the development prospects of the Sudan lies a basic question about the wisdom of differentiating sharply between relief and development assistance. However opprobrious the behavior of the political authorities, the lack of donor investment in increased food production had the effect of increasing people's vulnerability to famine. However difficult the accomplishment of development objectives while conflict continues, withholding longer-term assistance pending changed policies may itself be counterproductive. In fact, the downward trend in long-term aid noted earlier reduced the leverage of donors over objectionable policies.

In the Sudan during the late 1980s, the same governments that provided substantial emergency aid cut off all development and economic assistance to protest government policies. Withholding aid in the interests of influencing policy, however, had certain negative effects. Thorvald Stoltenberg, UN high commissioner for refugees, asked, "Should development assistance be linked to the human rights records of the recipient country? It may be tempting to say yes. But why should people in need be denied help because of their government's poor human rights record? That could make their situation even worse."[23] He might have posed the same question in regard to conditioning aid on human rights performance or on serious efforts at conflict resolution.

In a similar vein, the OEOA evaluation of emergency operations in neighboring Ethiopia noted that disenchantment with the policies of the government had not only reduced development assistance flows but also held up humanitarian aid itself. It chided donors for delaying, "at great cost of lives and great material losses, an operational effort which eventually it had to consent to, and could have foreseen as inescapable."[24]

One contributing factor in the Sudan was the concern of donor governments that existing agricultural policies were "counterproductive and bound to increase, rather than decrease, the dependence of the country on external support." As things turned out, the provision of exclusively emergency aid irritated the government and failed to produce the desired change in policies. The strategy of mounting massive humanitarian interventions on behalf of hungry people while denying them assistance toward self-reliance may well contribute to recurrent emergencies and end by costing more.

A more positive synergism between aid on the one hand and peace, human rights, and development concerns on the other is provided by the International Conference on Central American Refugees (CIREFCA), which was launched in Guatemala City in May 1989 with a three-year plan of action, subsequently extended through May 1994. The UN high commissioner for refugees, Sadako Ogata, recently described the CIREFCA approach and results, based on a political commitment to improve the stability of the region:

> Solutions for refugees and the internally displaced were . . . incorporated into the more durable process of peace and development. . . . The positive environment in which CIREFCA was born and which it has fostered in turn has led generally to the strengthening of protection for refugees in the region. On the other hand, the durability of the solutions depends on the extent to which refugee aid can be married to development assistance, and more importantly, to the overall resolution of the complex economic and social problems facing the Central American countries.[25]

Although Lifeline did not have establishing peace, protecting human rights, and promoting development as explicit objectives, each area clearly benefited from relief efforts. At the same time, the absence of conscious attention to the connections between relief operations and these interrelated areas meant that relief itself, however successful in operational terms, failed to achieve its full potential.

COORDINATING ACTIVITIES

Any major international emergency—be it a natural disaster, a crisis of human making, or some combination of the two—is certain nowadays to bring forth assistance from an overwhelming number of institutions and personnel. Coming in all sizes and shapes from diverse national and institutional backgrounds, these multifarious participants bring with them a multiplicity of bureaucratic and individual styles and a wide range of professional and personal views. They open headquarters and field offices, seek out hotel and private accommodations, organize transport fleets, install telephones and fax machines, and hire local professional and support staff.

Even before they set up shop, aid officials must interact with the host authorities on an array of policy and practical matters. They require a range of permissions, including contractual agreements authorizing their presence and outlining the scope and duration of their activities; visas and duty-free import agreements for relief supplies and personal effects; bank accounts and currency exchange arrangements; and permission to travel to the affected areas, preferably with priority seating on national air carriers and guaranteed fuel for their vehicles. Those who wish to undergird their operations with radio connections need special approval, particularly difficult to obtain in wartime.

This flurry of activity occurs at both national and local levels. In the case of Lifeline, the national-level activities took place in Khartoum for work in government-controlled areas and in Nairobi for areas within SPLA jurisdiction. In the SPLA's Kapoeta area in southeastern Equatoria Province, resident or itinerant expatriate relief workers in mid-1989 included staff members of UN agencies (primarily UNICEF and WFP), bilateral governments (such as the United States and the Netherlands), the ICRC, and private relief groups.

The largest single contingent of staff was from nongovernmental organizations. These included World Vision International (which was involved in programs of seed distribution, cattle vaccination, and medicine supply); the International Rescue Committee (supplementary feeding, immunization, and training of community health workers); Comité Internationale Médicale pour l'Urgence et Developpement and Lutheran World Relief (well drilling and maintenance of hand pumps); the African Medical and Research Foundation (training of health workers), Assistance Médicale International (primary health care); Oxfam-US (agriculture); and Street Kids International (education).

In addition to expatriate institutions, some of them represented by Sudanese personnel, the cast of characters included the political authorities: for the Sudanese government, members of the RRC, cabinet ministries, and regional and local government representatives; and for the SPLA, military commanders and the SRRA. Also present were indigenous Sudanese nongovernmental organizations such as Sudanaid (a Roman Catholic agency), the Sudan Council of Churches, the Sudan Red Crescent Society, and the Islamic African Relief Agency.

The ostensibly simple matter of tracking resources mobilized by and provided to Lifeline illustrates some of the technical difficulties of coordination. Resources originated with governments, UN agencies, and the public and were transmitted through a variety of institutions. Governments funded the activities of nongovernmental organizations and of UN agencies. The United Nations funded activities operated by the RRC and the SRRA and by international and indigenous NGOs. Some UN agencies received contributions from the general public. Some nongovernmental organizations gave funds and contributed personnel to UN agencies, to the RRC and the SRRA, and to indigenous NGOs. Simply avoiding double-counting was a major challenge. Variable fiscal years and lag time in reporting also conspired to make the amount of money available for the Sudan emergency difficult to determine.

If difficulties abounded in standardizing the flow of information from agencies associated with Lifeline, what of those operating to one degree or another independently of it? In 1989 the ICRC committed $70 million, and nongovernmental organizations substantial sums, to relief operations in the Sudan. These amounts benefited from UN appeals and were committed for activities consonant with Lifeline, but the implementing agencies were accountable to their own boards of directors and contributors, not to the United Nations. In short, there was no single point of information or reporting on all emergency operations.

The task of coordination, already difficult in the case of drought-induced famine, was enormously complicated by the civil war. The war confronted all aid providers with nettlesome problems. Could they assist needy people on both sides of the conflict as a means of confirming their humanitarian purposes? As that proved difficult, could they assist on only one side but in ways that did not confer political or military advantage? How could the safety of personnel be ensured in a conflict that required their presence?

Coordination difficulties were exacerbated by the diversity of the organizations. UN agencies generally functioned within the prevailing understanding of national sovereignty. That is, they operated as intergovernmental bodies comprising member states and representing government interests, political as well as humanitarian. They provided assistance at the request of and under terms negotiated with the government in charge.

Political constraints had a direct impact on humanitarian programs. In the period preceding Lifeline, the United Nations had acceded to pressure from the Sudan to recall UN personnel whose efforts to assist in the South had caused political problems with the Khartoum authorities. Donor members did not insist that the United Nations resist such pressure. In fact, they acquiesced in the expulsion of UN aid staff.The Lifeline agreement did not solve all such problems, though it did legitimize the functioning of UN programs and personnel in insurgent-controlled areas.

UNICEF has developed more latitude for operating in civil strife than many other UN agencies. Its involvement in the Sudan, as also in Afghanistan, Angola, Cambodia, El Salvador, Lebanon, Mozambique, and Sri Lanka, is understood to be purely humanitarian, conferring no political recognition on the armed opposition. In keeping with its traditions and de facto mandate, UNICEF deployed many staff members throughout the southern Sudan. Its readiness to deal with the insurgent political and military leadership to assist women and children represented a special contribution to the relief effort.

Other UN agencies lacked such authority. "The mandate of the UN in dealing with humanitarian needs in armed conflict settings needs to be fully legitimized and further strengthened," observed Michael Priestley in 1990 from his vantage point as manager of UN relief efforts, first in Ethiopia under the OEOA and then in the Sudan under Lifeline. "We're pushing at the frontiers right now. The issue of national sovereignty in circumstances of extreme human suffering due to conflict should be examined at UN headquarters with a view to expanding the secretary-general's powers."[26]

While the UN as an intergovernmental body responded to human need within the context of national sovereignty, some nongovernmental organizations took a different approach. While most sought to function within the terms set by the respective political authorities, many recognized claims to sovereignty only to the extent that they reflected humane values. "We are practitioners of what is possible rather than what is legal," remarked Marcus Thompson, emergency coordinator for Oxfam-UK.[27] At the same time, NGOs viewed their own activities as exerting pressure on governments to meet their acknowledged obligations under international humanitarian law.

Many nongovernmental organizations involved in relief operations in the southern Sudan welcomed the additional humanitarian space created by Lifeline, which enabled them to function more effectively. Yet they were intensely aware that what the warring parties had seen fit to grant in the 1989 Lifeline agreement, they might at some future point also retract—as indeed they did. The NGOs also remembered that in the years before Lifeline, the United Nations, reflecting political sensitivities, had itself explicitly discouraged efforts to reach those trapped by the war. "Let not the bias of the U.N.," said one private agency executive, "be the means of frustrating or constraining non-governmental organizations, which need not have that bias themselves."[28]

On issues of sovereign prerogatives and humanitarian obligations, donor governments adopted something of a middle ground. They were better able to respond to suffering than the United Nations but less able than the NGOs. In fact, the existence of Lifeline on the one hand and of nongovernmental groups on the other allowed governments to make a selection from among available aid channels based on the particulars of the moment.

"When donors are at odds with the recipient government," noted the UN's Michael Priestley, "they tend to put most of their resources through nongovernmental organizations and, at the same time, demand that the UN play a central coordinating role." As a result, he continued, "nongovernmental organizations have been deliberately used in cross-border operations where governments are either unwilling or unable to become directly involved. In most circumstances they do this with the full realization of the much reduced accountability that inevitably accompanies a strictly illicit operation."[29]

The U.S. government provides a case in point. Fearful throughout much of 1988 of offending the Sudanese government, the United States provided only a trickle of assistance to SPLA-controlled areas in the South—through private relief organizations operating from Kenya. As the suffering worsened and the United States sought to accelerate its aid, AID in late 1988 sent what it called a joint team to assess the needs there. The functioning of the team was hardly joint, since only its nongovernment members crossed into the South. Its report, however, became the basis for greater cross-border U.S. government aid flows. The United States also pressed the United Nations to initiate Lifeline and, thanks to the legitimacy it provided, then sent the first official U.S. relief personnel into the South.

In the context of the varying styles, accountabilities, and approaches to national sovereignty of the major relief organizations, the exercise of coordination involves political as well as technical complexities. Thus the same governments which demand that the UN ensure coordination pursue bilateral policies and practices that render such coordination difficult to provide. Indeed, based on the Sudan experience, it is not at all clear that any single agency or combination of agencies is best suited to provide coordination.

Perhaps the most that can be expected is a division of labor based on a common commitment to humanitarian principles and reflecting the distinctive contributions and comparative advantages of each agency. Achieving such an arrangement when natural disaster is involved is difficult enough; doing so in the context of a raging civil war is more difficult still.[30]

Assessing the need for relief provides another example of how the Sudan's civil war superimposed political difficulties upon problems that under normal circumstances would have been largely technical in nature. During the rushed preparations for the Khartoum conference in March 1989, the United Nations compiled background documents estimating emergency needs in the southern Sudan through November. The resulting Khartoum plan of action became a definitive statement on the magnitude of the crisis and the resources needed for dealing with it.

As it turned out, the UN assessment and the tonnage target based on it were not informed by first-hand information systematically gathered from insurgent-controlled areas in the South. In fact, papers prepared for the Khartoum conference studiously avoided mention of the SPLA by name, acknowledging that "little is known about the dispersed population which had managed to stay in its villages." Yet together with those displaced from their villages but remaining in areas under SPLA control, these people represented more than half of those in need of assistance.

For the United Nations, as for governments, insurgent-held territory had been terra incognita before Lifeline. Moreover, the Sudanese government had used security concerns to limit access to even government-held cities in the South. The UN assessment did not include information from the ICRC or from NGOs, which had staff members in the areas in question. Consequently, as in other civil conflicts in which the United Nations has had difficulty developing reliable data, relief operations themselves became, in the embarrassed euphemism of one official, "a voyage of discovery."[31]

At critical points throughout Lifeline, the absence of unimpeachable data complicated the task of allocating relief on the basis of need. In fact, one of the major recurring points of contention throughout Lifeline was the division of relief resources between the two sides. A mission by the FAO in late 1990 made an assessment that became the basis for the accepted estimates of food aid needed throughout the

Sudan in 1991. This assessment, too, failed to gather data firsthand from SPLA-controlled areas or government-held towns.

An important reason for coordination is the need to avoid waste and duplication and to contain costs. Relief efforts in 1989–91 provide a textbook illustration of how such costs, already high in 1984–86, escalated further still because of the conflict.

The war delayed the start of a large-scale relief intervention until April 1989. Working against the imminent return of the annual rains, aid officials then chose air transport as the major means for rushing aid to the more remote areas. The possibility that fighting might break out on some of the overland routes outside the corridors of tranquility contributed to the decision. However, air transportation increased the costs per ton per mile by a factor of as much as eight. In all, about 40 percent of Lifeline's 111,654 tons of food was moved by air. Costs escalated further still because of the SPLA's insistence that relief for its territory not be transshipped through Khartoum.

Program costs were also driven up by the need for special precautions against misappropriation. In mid-1989, more than forty officials posted around the South wearing UN arm bands were monitoring various points in the food chain. They rode at the head of relief convoys, negotiated with freight forwarders, and provided final checks on food distributions. UN staff members assigned full time to Lifeline totaled 175, an unusually intensive level of UN involvement. Moreover the climate of insecurity resulted in higher insurance costs on aid shipments and agency personnel. It also made what the United Nations termed "incentive payments" more extractable at various points along the way.

In effect, relief operations paid a civil war surcharge in virtually every expenditure category. The OEOA initiative had demonstrated that humanitarian activities in the Sudan were expensive even in the absence of conflict. With conflict added, costs escalated. Seasoned professionals have speculated that Sudan relief operations would rank among the most expensive of all operations that have been conducted during civil wars.

Such costs illuminate a number of related issues. First, while no expense is too great when lives are at stake, difficult questions of cost-effectiveness must be raised—later if not sooner. Second, the Sudan initiative had sizable opportunity costs that need to be evaluated. These include the trade-offs between spending resources on relief and making them available for longer-term development in the Sudan or for serious crises elsewhere. Third, a heavy influx of expensive outside assistance tends to make the host government less accountable to its own citizens and more answerable to outside governments and interests. While this may not be altogether negative on occasions when domestic authorities fail to acquit themselves of their responsibilities, the international community can itself prove a fickle partner.

In short, the coordination problems encountered during the drought-induced famine of 1983–86 were heightened during the conflict-related famine that followed. Moreover, the civil war also drove up the already high costs of operations, a condition that had serious implications for an effective and balanced program in the Sudan and elsewhere.

EVALUATING THE RESULTS

In its initial phase Lifeline helped bring down the curtain on the most devastating and searing humanitarian tragedy in modern Sudanese history. In 1989, it mobilized and deployed between $200 million and $300 million and provided international presence and pressure that eased the level of violence and brought a return to normalcy across large areas of the South. These are significant accomplishments.

With the return of the war in late 1989, however, problems at first contained soon worsened. A growing lack of cooperation from the warring parties, reflecting an upsurge in political and military tension, combined with weaknesses in Lifeline itself to sacrifice much of the ground gained earlier. While the humanitarian principles on which Lifeline was built were never explicitly retracted, they were subjected to almost daily battering. The recurrence of serious, though localized, food shortages in the South and of major shortages in the North provided fresh cause for alarm. Consequently, Lifeline's results were mixed.

Perhaps the most fundamental question to be asked in evaluating those results is whether those whose suffering was the object of relief operations are better off because of them. Are they now more self-reliant, or more dependent on outside resources?

The situation of the population of Juba has changed very little since

1988; the city has remained under siege throughout. During this time the day-to-day needs of the people have been met by an airlift from Nairobi, which began in November 1988 under the auspices of the Lutheran World Federation (LWF) shortly after it was expelled from Khartoum. The airlift was underwritten by funds from church organizations and supplemented by contributions from other nongovernmental sources, governments, and UN agencies. By 1991 it had cost $35 million—almost $1,000 per ton of supplies transported. Once relief items arrived in Juba, they were distributed effectively by a consortium of NGOs, the Combined Agencies Relief Team (CART).

The airlift also transported aid personnel into the South and evacuated them when the situation became perilous. Most expatriates left Juba in January 1990, when increased SPLA military activity hit the UN compound and hospital, an NGO project, and a camp for displaced persons. At various times the airlift was interrupted, sometimes by a ban on flights imposed by the government and sometimes by SPLA threats to shoot. LWF generally succeeded in starting it up again with a minimum of delay. The airlift deserves credit for helping to keep the civilian population alive, a sizable accomplishment in itself. It also made a major contribution to the psychological well-being of the residents.

Nevertheless, LWF decided that, beginning in July 1991, it would no longer operate the airlift. The change of approach reflected its sense that the plight of the people of Juba had remained basically unchanged, the cause of their suffering unaddressed, and precious resources diverted from other activities that might have had more durable benefits. There was even an uneasy feeling that the airlift might be decreasing the pressure on the warring parties to resolve their differences. Certainly, the absence of the airlift would lend additional urgency to winning agreement from both sides to open up cheaper overland routes into Juba from Kenya and Uganda.

The situation on the ground supported this view. Throughout these years, the civilian population of Juba was held twice-hostage: by an inner circle of government troops, itself surrounded by an outer circle of insurgent forces. The number of hostages—both sides claim that civilians have been free to leave—is thought to have remained roughly constant throughout. The number of those who have managed to thread their way through the minefields back to the countryside has probably somewhat exceeded the number of those who have found their way into Juba, seeking whatever security the encircled city may provide.

Even the size of the population of Juba has been in dispute, estimates varying from as low as 30,000 to as high as 500,000. Whatever the number, food was in such short supply in mid-1991 that nongovernmental organizations, joined on this occasion by the Sudan government, appealed once again for international help to avoid imminent famine.

Among those particularly vulnerable within the city were some 5,500 members of the Toposa tribe. A UNICEF report noted in mid-1991 that "many are without clothing, shelter or food. They are starving to death. Most appear to be suffering from diarrhoea, TB and pneumonia. It is estimated that 400 boys under 18 years of age are among these tribesmen." Efforts were being mounted to provide the tribe with food and medicine on an emergency basis.[32]

Easing the plight of Juba's civilians was the centerpiece of a plan the U.S. government proposed in June 1991. Assistant Secretary of State Herman Cohen called on both sides to declare Juba an open city. The government, which would still control the city, would withdraw most of its troops, leaving behind a civilian administrator. Encircling SPLA troops would pull back about seventy-five miles and scrap plans to capture the city. Cohen's proposal was intended, he explained, as "a dramatic gesture which would both improve the lives of many Sudanese and perhaps build confidence among both the government and the SPLA that peace is an option." On the humanitarian side, it would "allow food convoys and normal trade to move unrestricted," removing the need for the "horrendously expensive airlift." On the political side, it would remove Juba as an object of conflict. "If peace can work here," Cohen observed, "it can work in other areas of Sudan."

The proposal received mixed reviews. Initially a Sudanese government official opposed it, although the government subsequently warmed to the idea. The SPLA suspected that it would be forced to make disproportionate concessions. As a result, the initiative was stillborn. Juba remains the graveyard not only of many southern Sudanese but also of many plans to assist them. Juba's civilians, rather than being better off than before the relief interventions, are now more vulnerable. In late 1991 there was even speculation that the SPLA might soon attempt to take Juba, seeking to recover the stature it lost when it was expelled from its bases in Ethiopia with the fall of Mengistu. Thus the ambivalence of relief operations: notwithstanding millions of dollars and immeasurable energy invested, most of Juba's civilians are alive but vulnerable.[33]

What of the population in the countryside controlled by the insurgents? A comparison of the situation in Leer when Lifeline was launched with that two years later is instructive, if disconcerting. Leer is a small and isolated rural district in Upper Nile Province, which suffered greatly during the tragic year of 1988. The condition of the people there stunned the first UN officials to visit the area in early 1989. "There was a look on people's faces of desolation and shock—as if years of war and suffering had left them numb with the horror of it all," recalled Patta Smith-Villers of Lifeline. "We saw the same look everywhere we went."

As a result, Leer became one of several primary targets for relief operations. The area received sizable assistance from a wide range of UN and other aid agencies. Returning to the area after several months of intensive relief efforts, Smith-Villers marveled at what she saw. "I had only to think of the change in the look on people's faces to know that the [relief] work was worthwhile. People were once again able to smile. We had helped to bring a sense of normality and security just by our presence."[34] Her recollection brightened a period in April 1990 when relief efforts in Leer and elsewhere in areas controlled by the SPLA were floundering and morale among the relief personnel was sagging.

The report of the AID mission that visited the area a year later suggests that many of the difficulties persisted. The team found "an immediate and critical need for seeds and food in Leer," which had been without relief assistance since the previous year. Malnutrition and kala-azar were widespread among children and adults. "Although small amounts of grain are currently available from Leek—a five-day round trip from Leer—it is clear that grain supplies are extremely scarce, that many families cannot afford grain at any price, and that seed grain has largely been consumed as food." In observations reminiscent of those made in 1989 and 1990, the team noted that rains were preventing transportation of relief supplies by road and that a nearby barge was idled awaiting repairs.[35]

The situation in Leer is probably not typical of the rural countryside, where normalcy may have returned to a greater degree. On the other hand, many of the other locations for which the AID team expressed concern—Nasir, Akon, Yirol, Ayod, Waat, Akobo, and Pibor—had also been the subject of earlier Lifeline efforts. Even if some of those in need were among the recent influx of returnees from Ethiopia, it still seems reasonable to conclude that many people in the SPLA-controlled rural countryside remain in perilous circumstances and dependent on continued international relief.[36]

Similarly, little positive change can be reported in the situation of a third major population group: people displaced from the South who sought refuge around Khartoum. "The numbers of displaced by war and drought in Khartoum is believed to be between 1 and 2 million," reported AID in mid-1991. The report makes the alarming observation that "a large number of displaced persons in Khartoum may be left over from the 1984–85 drought." Others had fled from the more recent violence and food shortages in the southern province of Bahr el Ghazal.

While exact figures are unavailable, the displaced population in Khartoum and its outskirts appears to have remained in the range of 1 million to 2 million during 1989–91, despite government efforts to resettle people in their areas of origin. "The last move began in early June and resulted in the complete relocation of 2,000 families," noted AID in 1991. Yet questions have been raised about poor preparation of reception facilities and possible coercion to move. "The U.N. is greatly concerned about the adequacy of shelter and sanitation at the Jebel Awelia camp, [warning] of an impending cholera epidemic . . . due to completely insufficient sanitation facilities." The government has also announced plans to relocate back to Kordofan some 20,000 persons from around Khartoum.[37] In late 1991 and the first six months of 1992, the government pressed ahead with the relocation of substantial numbers of people.

A second and related question concerning the results of emergency operations has to do with their effects on the attitudes of the opposing parties in the civil war. A comparison of sentiments throughout the period of the conflict-related aid intervention suggests that both sides became more sensitive to international opinion but were no less committed to pursuing their bitter struggle by military means. In fact, after the initial six months of Lifeline operations, military operations became the major preoccupation of both warring parties.

A comparison of two visits to Washington by SPLA commander

John Garang is instructive. In June 1989 he arrived fresh from a string of military victories and was enjoying the enhanced recognition conferred by his cooperation in Lifeline. U.S. government officials gave him a friendly reception. When U.S. nongovernmental organizations appealed for the safety of the citizens of Juba, Garang replied matter-of-factly, "If I can take Juba, I will take Juba." At the same time, he expressed the SPLA's commitment to abide by the letter and spirit of the Geneva Conventions and Protocols and to protect civilians from indiscriminate warfare.

When Garang returned to Washington in June 1991, the scene had changed. He had no recent battlefield successes to report; international patience with the obstacles encountered by relief operations was wearing thin. A recurring question concerned the relocation of SPLA command centers and camps from Ethiopia following the demise of Mengistu. Denying that SPLA headquarters had ever been in Ethiopia, Garang stated that the insurgents had many friends in the region and would have no trouble making alternative arrangements to continue the struggle. Reminded of the plight of Juba's civilians, Garang said that for strategic and tactical as well as humanitarian reasons, he had ordered his troops not to fire on Juba. He recalled that he himself had offered to allow international monitors to accompany Juba hostages back to their homes in the countryside. The SPLA and the government alike continued to insist that civilians remain in the encircled city only because of the actions of the other party.

Garang claimed that the SPLA was continuing to cooperate with relief groups, while Khartoum obstructed their efforts. He enthusiastically endorsed the idea of diverting funds from the Juba airlift to reconstruction and development activities in the South but stopped short of assurances that land corridors would be opened to allow relief convoys to reach Juba by road instead. In fact, he bristled at the news that the Khartoum authorities had agreed to overland access. It is not theirs to grant, he said. The capture of Juba seemed to remain a military objective for the SPLA.

Garang was asked if the recent experience in Ethiopia did not suggest that the SPLA should invest energies in peace instead of relocating its bases elsewhere and digging in for a protracted military struggle. The lesson from the Eritrean struggle, Garang answered, was that some wars require thirty years. Given the importance of military objectives, concern about the continued human suffering becomes a secondary consideration. In fact, because of the tensions between the Sudanese insurgents and the liberation movements in Ethiopia, efforts to encourage a meeting between the SPLA and the new Ethiopian regime, which might have avoided the need for southern Sudanese to leave Ethiopia after the fall of Mengistu, were not taken seriously. Humanitarian concerns and international pressure seem in this instance to have had very limited influence on the decisionmaking of the warring parties.

In both Washington visits, Garang summoned up considerable eloquence to make his case. "At the end of the day," he said he told Cohen in responding to the proposal that Juba become an open city, "peace is the best relief activity." The stunning truth of his statement failed to mask the fact that at the end of more than one thousand days of relief activity, widespread suffering continued, and peace seemed as remote as ever. Whether the war will ultimately accomplish its stated political objectives and bring benefits to the civilian population remains debatable. It is clear, however, that there can be no lasting peace in the South without justice and equality for all citizens, irrespective of race or religion, an eventuality that seems remote under the present circumstances of fundamentalist Islamic rule.

The reversion of the SPLA position to almost pre-Lifeline contours reflects a similar retrenchment on the part of the government in Khartoum. This toughened approach appears to reflect a combination of pressure from Muslim fundamentalists associated with the National Islamic Front, deepening national economic woes, and increased isolation following the regime's identification with Iraq during the 1991 Gulf War. Once again, stepped-up rhetorical endorsements of peace by the government in Khartoum have resulted in few concrete initiatives to moderate or end the conflict.

The implications for humanitarian concerns are heavily negative, as illustrated by an incident at the Sudan conference in Washington in June 1991, at which the Cohen proposal was unveiled. A speaker noted that the Sudan government's recent appeal for help in coping with the influx of refugees from Ethiopia fleeing the new regime coincided with eye-witness reports of bombing in the Sudan and Ethiopia by the Sudan government of southern Sudanese who, caught in the same upheaval, were returning to the southern Sudan. How could the same government, the speaker asked, request humanitarian assistance for the Ethiopians while bombing its own citizens?

The returnees, a senior government official asserted in response, were insurgents who had fled to Ethiopia when the Sudan's civil war heated up and were now returning in fear. On the other hand, the Ethiopians seeking asylum in the Sudan were a different case altogether. Political and military officials associated with the Mengistu regime and their families, unlike the insurgents, had a legitimate claim on humanitarian aid.

Tortured distinctions notwithstanding, the situation was itself complex. While the influx of returnees from Ethiopia came largely from refugee camps such as Itang and Fugnido, where the SPLA had housed not only refugees but military trainees, most of the people returning were themselves civilians. (Had they all been soldiers, Garang later joked, he would have had enough troops to take Khartoum.) However, as civilians, they had rights deserving of respect by political authorities, a respect not conveyed in the official attitude. The missing sense of humanity is, in fact, what Lifeline had sought to establish.

In general, the government appeared during much of 1991 somewhat more solicitous of international public opinion and more anxious to plead its case persuasively. Those desires figured in its hosting the conference in Washington in June 1991 to provide a platform for explaining its views and in the appearance of President Bashir at the UN Summit for Children in New York in September 1990, where he endorsed the new treaty and announced several new programs. Much of the rhetoric remained cosmetic, however, disembodied from validating actions with tangible benefits for vulnerable people. Both sides remained staunchly committed to incompatible national visions and objectives.

Did emergency operations in the Sudan in 1987–91 serve the cause of humanitarian values internationally? Even granted the dilemmas and ambiguities examined, this question deserves an affirmative answer. One of the conclusions of the Lifeline study was that the initiative succeeded in establishing the basic humanitarian principle that civilians in civil wars have a fundamental right to assistance and that the international community has a companion right to provide it. In the words of one relief official, "The principle is the best part of Operation Lifeline Sudan."[38] That principle was worth affirming, even though at some points humanitarian values might have been better served by a cessation than by a continuation of relief assistance. As a matter of principle, not to have responded to human need, however daunting the circumstances, would have been unconscionable. That was the course initially taken in the Liberian civil war and in postwar Iraq.

Whatever the frustrations and disappointments of Lifeline within the Sudan, its basic principles and some of its operational procedures have already had important precedent-setting value, as both protagonists regularly point out. Some of the personnel associated with Lifeline have been made available to similar initiatives in Angola and Ethiopia. Institutions involved in the Sudan—UN agencies, governments, and NGOs alike—have begun to distill their experiences in the interest of improving future operations.

In historical context, Lifeline was a prominent part of a larger effort by the international community, now gathering momentum, to deal creatively with political constraints such as sovereignty and with the operational unwieldiness of the aid system in order to avert famine deaths and alleviate other preventable suffering. Because the terrain in the Sudan was so treacherous, it was to be expected that the experience itself would be uneven. The difficulties simply underscored the urgency and raised the stakes for success.

It would be premature, however, to conclude that the lessons have been fully learned, much less adequately applied, either to the continuing difficulties in the Sudan or to other conflict situations. Relief operations in the Sudan late in the decade repeated some of the mistakes of the 1984–86 period. Morevoer, difficulties identified in the early phases of Lifeline still impair its effectiveness. Thunderclouds remain over the Sudan even as the humanitarian horizon elsewhere is brightening.

Chapter 4

A Look to the Future

At the end of 1991, the international community was still wrestling with the problems of emergency humanitarian operations dramatized in the Sudan and confirmed by experience elsewhere. Some reflections on the challenges these problems pose for the future are in order, along with some recommendations for action.

THE GENERIC PROBLEMS IN PERSPECTIVE

The first problem illuminated by the Sudan experience has to do with the external nature of emergency relief operations. National leaders tend to perceive humanitarian intervention as an exposure of their failure to find effective remedies to the plight of their people, an insult to their national pride, and an intercession on behalf of a segment of the population with which they often do not fully identify. While this problem is likely to remain an obstacle to humanitarian assistance for the foreseeable future, there are ways of minimizing the externalities of aid interventions.

In the case of emergencies induced by natural disasters, this obstacle may be dealt with by more sensitive and open discussion between the authorities and the donor community. Pressure from outside may well be necessary, but with appropriate sensitivity to the concerns of the government, national leadership, and domestic public opinion, it should be possible to foster a style of interaction and cooperation that reduces the intrusive aspects of the requisite intervention.

In the case of emergencies that are related to conflict, the gulf separating the victims from the holders of state power and the armed opposition is greater and more highly charged. When leaders are unwilling to accept responsibility for the survival and general welfare of a part of their own people, the international community must step forward as advocates of the people, even assuming direct, if temporary, responsibility for them. This requires dealing effectively with the warring parties simultaneously, a delicate diplomatic task.

In the Sudan, a fortunate confluence of political, military, and humanitarian factors encouraged both parties to consent to the initial intervention, even though their consent was in constant danger of being withdrawn. Such confluence may not always be present or such consent be possible. Saving lives must be the paramount objective, however. The international community must be willing to override the resistance of political authorities to intervention on behalf of a threatened group of people when the magnitude and extremity of the crisis justifies such action. Under no circumstances should the world countenance massive starvation of the kind the Sudan experienced in 1988, when an estimated quarter of a million people were allowed to starve to death. For such situations, criteria and mechanisms should be devised that put greater, but also carefully circumscribed, coercive power in the service of humanitarian interests.

The second problem, that of context—in which preoccupations with short-term emergency aid supersede longer-term rehabilitation and development concerns—is inherent in all humanitarian emergencies, whether natural or human in origin. In the latter instance, the problem is often complicated by the slow pace with which emergencies are detected, the reluctance of political authorities to acknowledge crises and request assistance, and the belatedness with which the donor community frequently responds. Emergency operations could be much smoother and better proportioned if early warning systems were available to activate the necessary responses. Such an approach would require more systematic attention to local social and economic indicators of distress, more adequate reserves of emergency supplies either already in place or more readily summoned, more responsible leadership in vulnerable countries, and more flexible procedures on the part of the agencies providing assistance.

Improved arrangements would take into account the reality that the donor community, under the pressure of public opinion, usually moves to mobilize relief operations only when a given crisis is well advanced. Better foresight and longer-term planning would deprive emergency situations of their compelling urgency and reduce the sense of panic engendered by circumstances that are already out of control.

Costs would also be contained by improved early warning and early response systems, which would help avoid the need for air transportation of relief supplies and other expensive measures. A more concerted, sustainable global strategy for confronting emergencies that included among its elements greater standby authority and more resources for multilateral agencies would also reduce the current dependence of international responses on sensational and uneven media coverage.

Although the all-hands-on-deck nature of emergency action does not lend itself to addressing the related issues of development, human rights, and peace, those interconnections cannot be ignored. Lifeline operations in 1989 demonstrated that shifting over at the earliest possible moment from providing food for immediate consumption to supplying seeds to produce food locally represented not only a saving in bulk transportation costs but an investment in a more self-reliant future. At the same time, the failure to resolve the underlying conflict made reinvigorated agricultural productivity vulnerable to renewed hostilities.

The third problem, concerning coordination as an essential but often unwanted aspect of emergency operations, also calls for improved international cooperation. While the United Nations is widely recognized as the most likely coordinating vehicle, its nature as an organization of governments compromises its objectivity when the behavior of a given member state is in question. This was less of a problem, although still a significant constraint, when the OEOA sought to deal with the drought-induced emergency. In the case of Lifeline, the natural bias of the United Nations toward governments and its discomfort in dealing with insurgencies impeded its effective exercise of coordination.

Even when multilateral coordinating machinery is functioning effectively, governments, nongovernmental organizations, and the international media have key roles to play. The Sudan experience indicates that donors such as the United States may both facilitate and hamper UN efforts. It also suggests that NGOs—which in both kinds of famines functioned by and large as an effective, if largely unheeded, early warning system—should not have their activities unduly constrained by the coordinating efforts of governments. At the same time, private aid groups need to enhance the professionalism and collegiality of their own functioning in both sets of circumstances. A more studied division of labor among all participants is clearly in order.

The fourth problem, which concerns the ambivalent results of emergency operations will most likely vary according to the cause of the emergency. Famine resulting from a natural disaster is likely to be limited for the most part to the duration of the disaster itself. The dependence of the people affected is therefore likely to be circumscribed in space and time, unless a sequence of back-to-back crises creates such environmental and social havoc that the natural setting and society are slow to recover. Following an isolated famine, populations temporarily dislocated may return to their original homes. Recurrent famines make such a return more difficult.

Conflict-related emergencies increase the dangers of dependency, reflecting both the intensity and the longevity of the strife. As long as recipients of emergency relief remain cut off from their natural resource base and prohibited from exercising self-reliance, they remain vulnerable to continued dependency. The warring parties in the Sudan have made the dislocation of civilians from their traditional agricultural and economic pursuits an all-too-successful instrument of political and military policy.

Satisfactory results from relief operations must combine emergency assistance with rehabilitation of the victims in self-sustaining occupations, especially in agriculture. The OEOA and Lifeline experiences alike highlight a troubling lack of attention both to involving the people and their local institutions and to surrounding the relief activities with a supportive context in which self-reliance may soon flourish once again.

This review of the experiences of two major international interventions within a single decade in a single country also provides striking—and distressing—evidence of the limited extent to which the results of past efforts inform future relief activities. The encouragement by UN and other aid agencies of the two studies reviewed in this volume indicates an awareness of the need to distill the lessons to be learned from major initiatives. A more extended review of the experiences of humanitarian interventions in other civil war settings is currently in progress.[1] In only the most narrow and almost coincidental of ways, however, did the planning of Lifeline bear any considered relationship to the OEOA experience.

NEW HORIZONS ON HUMANITARIAN IMPERATIVES

During both the drought-induced and the conflict-related interventions in the Sudan, humanitarian interests were at odds with political authorities who failed to meet obligations to their populations and refused to allow others to do so. Successive regimes in Khartoum as well as the insurgents in the South declined to feed the people within their respective jurisdictions or even to recognize their serious food needs and call for international assistance.

Such indifference to the plight of people threatened with starvation is, of course, not new. It contributed to the downfall of the emperor in Ethiopia and probably also to President Nimeiri's fall from power in the Sudan. While such indifference raises sensitive political issues of sovereignty, including the political will of the people in choosing, tolerating, or removing their leaders, an issue of fundamental human rights is involved that transcends the boundaries of sovereign states.

Understandings of sovereignty are changing. The balance between sovereignty and suffering is shifting in favor of greater international sensitivity to the claims of those who suffer and greater impatience with the obstructionism of uncaring governments. This evolution in part reflects the experience of Lifeline and other recent international initiatives that have successfully prevailed on political authorities to allow relief activities. Even more, however, it is a product of recent dramatic events in the Gulf.

The response of the world community to the plight of the Iraqi Kurds and Shiites following the Gulf War upgraded the importance of responding to suffering and challenged the assumption that repressive governments should be allowed to abuse their civilian populations with impunity. In resolution 688, adopted on April 5, 1991, the United Nations Security Council for the first time in history determined that humanitarian suffering *within* a given member state was a threat to *international* peace and security. It insisted that the Iraqi government "allow immediate access by international organizations to all those in need of assistance" and requested the secretary-general to see that such aid was provided.

The situation to which the Security Council responded was unusual. In a series of broadly supported resolutions beginning in August 1990, the council had authorized economic and other necessary action against the Iraqi government to bring about its withdrawal from Kuwait. As a result, there was a clearer sense after the war of international responsibility to attend to the conflict's serious human consequences. In other respects, however, the proposition that international protection and assistance should be extended to a group whose welfare is deemed important to international peace and security has far-reaching implications.

Situations such as those in Iraq and in the Sudan dramatize the need for positive intervention by the world community where necessary to persuade governments to permit relief. The instincts of a world that has demonstrated increasing solidarity in support of the lofty ideals of humanitarianism are now less willing to allow governments and insurgencies to place at risk the lives of their citizens. Moreover, the international political climate is now more amenable to putting in place procedures that will bring pressure and leverage to bear in the interests of those who suffer.[2]

NEEDED INSTITUTIONAL REFORMS

The reviews of the OEOA and Lifeline experiences contained numerous recommendations for making emergency relief operations more effective. The present moment is propitious for their adoption.

First, *establish a mechanism to ensure high-level international political review of humanitarian emergencies.* Currently, there is no guarantee that emerging or existing situations of significant human suffering will be brought before the United Nations. The reluctance of the Sudan government to confront such situations delayed joint action in both 1983–84 and 1988, when the tragedies were gathering momentum and other governments, for their own reasons, did not take the initiative. In fact, both instances demonstrated what the Ethiopia evaluation termed a "lack of dynamism in the U.N. system and the relative indifference in the donor community as a whole."[3]

Almost four years before the humanitarian intervention in Iraq, the evaluation of OEOA relief operations in Ethiopia had called for developing techniques to enable the UN system to act, "at least in the first stage, independently of governments."[4] Several months before the Gulf crisis the Lifeline study had recommended a "humanitarian trigger mechanism [to] automatically bring an acute civil war situation to the attention of the Security Council." Such a mechanism would counter the reluctance of governments, insurgent groups, members of the UN Secretariat, and even the secretary-general to address humanitarian issues of major political consequence. Factors that might require automatic Security Council review of a natural or human-caused disaster could include the number of persons affected, the severity of the threat to human life, the generation of substantial human displacement, an emerging pattern of significant human rights violations, or the demonstrated inability of the government to cope with the crisis.

The urgency of putting into place such a mechanism is dramatized by the fact that the Security Council's preoccupation with the situation in Iraq blunted efforts in August 1990 to bring the critical needs of people in Liberia to its attention. Provisions are needed to force a humanitarian crisis of such magnitude onto the Security Council agenda. Had such provisions been in place in 1984 and 1988, the lives of countless Sudanese might have been spared.

Formulating ground rules for such review, and for humanitarian intervention itself, would put governments on notice, broaden the consensual basis for action, and narrow the remaining situations in which political authorities have to be overridden. In such a process, essential roles need to be played by host governments and armed opposition groups, other governments, intergovernmental organizations and UN agencies, nongovernmental organizations, academics, concerned citizens, and the media. Carefully constructed and consultatively pursued, the process itself could be an occasion for addressing some of the legitimate and well-grounded fears among developing countries regarding arbitrary, selective, and politically motivated interventions.

Agreed-upon ground rules would mandate only review by the Security Council, not UN intervention in each instance. Such an exercise, and the implementation of procedures that emerge from it, would need to be permeated by both a sensitivity to the various points of view respecting emergency situations and the overriding imperative of saving lives. Negotiating these principles before an emergency developed would enhance their chances of being implemented under duress.

For example, most governments have at one point or another been involved in or supported a cross-border operation to provide aid to a vulnerable population in another country. A majority of governments might therefore support the proposition that cross-border initiatives are a legitimate device for ensuring compliance with recognized humanitarian principles. That would leave only the particulars of a situation to be debated. This and other devices would encourage a more automatic response. One positive development along these lines was the adoption by the UN General Assembly in December 1991 of a resolution (46-182) that endorses strategies such as cross-border operations and corridors of tranquility.

Second, *develop a code of conduct to encourage higher levels of professionalism among aid providers*. Both emergencies in the Sudan tested the ability of aid institutions of all kinds to function effectively and revealed deficiencies in the institutions in the areas of professionalism within and collegiality among them.

The extent of human need in the Sudan drew aid agencies into activities of an uncharacteristic nature and scale. In the OEOA effort, this was particularly a problem for NGOs, whose involvement on a scale normally associated with governments and UN agencies created difficulties for them. In the Lifeline initiative, it was particularly a problem for UN organizations, whose emergency activities assumed an uncharacteristically operational and personnel-intensive character. In the civil war, the fact that NGOs were not familiar with applicable humanitarian law was an area of particular weakness.

Despite the differences between the two types of emergencies, the recommendations offered by the team that reviewed Lifeline are appropriate to the earlier intervention as well. They include developing a cadre of experienced staff members for rapid deployment; cultivating greater familiarity with contextual considerations (political and economic, religious and cultural); and exercising greater prudence and vigilance against becoming overextended. A number of efforts to develop codes of conduct are currently under way.[5]

Third, *foster a stricter sense of proportionality and balance*. A recurring problem of emergency operations throughout the decade was achieving the requisite fine-tuning of relief interventions at times when the crisis placed a premium on responding quickly to burgeoning needs. Balance was a problem not only within the Sudan operations but between efforts in the Sudan and in other emergencies.

The OEOA succeeded in molding a series of improvised international responses to individual country crises into a coordinated effort throughout sub-Saharan Africa. For this reason, the study of the OEOA recommended that its structure, or at least its function, be continued. The absence of such a mechanism later in the decade helped account for the fact that serious food shortages in nations such as Somalia and Mozambique received short shrift when the attention of the world was focused on the Sudan.

Both studies noted the critical role played by the media in sounding the international alarm and in helping to mobilize resources. As in Ethiopia in 1984, the media in both emergencies in the Sudan were the catalyst for action. Media attention, however, proved to be uneven and unpredictable.

With such considerations in mind, the Lifeline review recommended establishing a high-level focal point within the United Nations system, perhaps in the form of a new under-secretary-general for humanitarian affairs. The report recalled the contributions of the OEOA, which had promoted cooperation between the UN system and nongovernmental organizations, facilitated the gathering and dissemination of information, supported the mobilization of extraordinary resources, and helped expedite aid delivery—all areas in which Lifeline itself had experienced difficulty. The creation in early 1992 of a Department of Humanitarian Affairs, headed by an under secretary general, is a step in the direction recommended.

Fourth, *focus more attention on institution building and indigenous resourcefulness.* Both reviews noted the foreign character not only of the resources provided but of the personnel administering them. The OEOA study also commented on the disparity between the relative privilege of the expatriate relief staff and the deprivation of the indigenous population. Many expatriate staff members enjoyed living conditions that were not commensurate with their low level of expertise and experience. The absence of attention to training was also criticized. Prime Minister Gazouli Dafulla observed, "The more you involve the people, the more you train them, the more you get out of it and the more you guard against such a [crisis] situation arising." The Lifeline study found many of these difficulties recurring. Noting the "predominantly western ownership and style" of Lifeline, the report concluded that greater efforts should have been made to enlist the involvement of indigenous NGOs and media in the relief program.

The thrust of both reviews is that emergency operations should maintain a more discreet international profile. On the one hand, expatriate presence facilitates international cooperation and helps to interject innovation, efficiency, and experience gained in other crises. On the other hand, nationals and expatriates must be able to work together in all phases of emergency operations and development cooperation. A more sensitive approach would be to reinforce the resourcefulness of indigenous populations and to capitalize on proven survival techniques. Particular attention should be given to selecting expatriate staff in terms not only of the technical expertise required but also of the ability to manage human relationships in cross-cultural situations.

Fifth, *establish clearer authority for UN agencies to deal with armed insurgencies on humanitarian issues.* The normal problems of humanitarian interventions noted in the OEOA study were complicated by the civil war later in the decade. Where the OEOA had only a single set of government officials to relate to, Lifeline had two: the authorities in Khartoum and the Sudan People's Liberation Army. The civil war complicated the coordination and flow of information. It also reinforced the bias of the UN system in favor of member governments and made it difficult to deal with the warring parties on an impartial basis. The exigencies of the civil war also magnified problems between and among the UN specialized agencies.

In order to mount and maintain effective operations in settings torn by civil strife, the United Nations and its component parts need clearer authority to provide assistance and protection across conflict lines. The mandate to deal with insurgent groups on humanitarian matters without conferring recognition or legitimacy upon them, a mandate enjoyed only by UNICEF and, more recently, by the World Food Program, should be broadened to include other key agencies such as the High Commission for Refugees and indeed the UN system as a whole.

One means of ensuring greater responsiveness would be to provide for greater multilateral initiative. Earlier reference to the OEOA study of Ethiopia noted its recommendation that the UN system be empowered to act, "at least in the first stage, independently of donor governments." Such independence will not be welcomed by governments that have traditionally kept UN agencies on a short leash. More effective response to human need, however, will require that UN agencies assume greater latitude for action within agreed terms of reference. The capacity of NGOs to act independently of political constraints would benefit from strengthening as well.

RELIEF AND THE PROSPECTS FOR PEACE

A pertinent question for the future, a time in which civil strife is likely to occur in many nations, concerns whether relief impedes or promotes the cause of peace. The Sudan experience indicates that it does both. A moral imperative, providing aid cannot be compromised for political considerations. However, it can promote the prospects of peace, which is the ultimate solution to the tragedy of conflict-related famine.

Emergency relief mitigates the suffering of civilian populations caused by war. Since the civilian populations cannot be isolated from the conflict, especially in the case of guerrilla wars, both the consequences of war and the amelioration provided by emergency relief are broadly shared between the armies and the civilians. Mitigating the suffering may make war more tolerable and therefore more sustainable, as probably occurred in the Sudan in 1990–91. Motivated by the continuation of suffering, even on a reduced scale, and by the frustration of the prospects for development, those providing relief should also be committed to bringing about peace as soon as possible.

Those who provide emergency relief cannot be expected to go on doing so indefinitely. They, too, have an interest in an early end to the emergency. This is especially true when "aid fatigue" makes it increasingly difficult to generate sustained commitments of resources for emergency assistance. Those providing assistance thus often find it necessary to concern themselves with the prospects for peace, if not to mediate directly between the warring parties.

Dependency-inducing results are far more likely to be associated with conflict-related emergencies, which tend to be more open ended. Uncertainties about the end of the conflict leave the displaced neither comfortable with the thought of relocating permanently nor able to predict when peace might allow them to return home. The most viable solution in such circumstances is to negotiate their security with the warring factions, perhaps resettling those interested as close as possible to their natural settings but outside the zone of conflict.

With these considerations in mind, one of the co-authors, Francis Deng, in November 1988 proposed the establishment of Peace Havens in the southern Sudan.[5] The proposal sought to address the terrorization of the rural population by the Arab militias and the resulting moral catastrophe experienced by southern tribes in the transition zone between the northern and southern Sudan.

"Noted for their intense pride in their ethnic and cultural identity, their cattle wealth, and the productivity of their fertile soil," the proposal observed, the Dinka and Nuer of the South had been dislodged by the war from their natural habitat and "rendered incapable of supporting themselves." Building on the interest in the return of peace that they shared with the Arab Baggara of the North despite historic animosities, the proposal appealed for an international effort "to convince all parties to agree on designating certain areas of the South as Peace Havens in which those members of the civilian population desiring nothing but peace might be settled and provided with life-supporting necessities."

While the proposal was initially considered unrealistic, the protection of ethnic, religious, and other minorities endangered by conflict and alienated from a hostile government is now increasingly a recognized obligation of the international community. The establishment in 1991 of UN-sanctioned enclaves for the Kurds in northern Iraq has put flesh on international obligations. The next step is to develop principles and operational mechanisms to make such protection more widely available across a range of settings.

In the Sudan, Arab and Dinka tribes have succeeded in the intervening years, albeit tenuously, in working out arrangements to return to peaceful coexistence and to their traditional practices of cultivation and cooperative herding. The SPLA has called the outcome "a beautiful development," perhaps in part because it marks a shift in tactics by northern tribes, which shows increasing respect for SPLA power.

The development also reflects a corresponding distancing from the military government in Khartoum, which is hostile to the sectarian political parties. This is particularly true in the case of al-Mahdi's Umma party, whose traditional base of support is among the Arab tribes of western Sudan bordering the South. This conciliatory trend further suggests that whatever the interests of the government and the SPLA in keeping the conflict alive, local groups, left to their own devices, can sometimes find pragmatic resolutions of their differences based on their need to live together.

The experiences of the Sudan and Iraq also indicate the close interconnection between the short-term humanitarian and human rights agendas on the one hand and the longer-term causes of peace, security, stability, and development on the other. Although those concerned with the former generally avoid getting directly involved in the latter, most recognize that the ideal solution to conflict-related famine is an end to the conflict itself. And while humanitarian intervention is different from peacemaking, the discussion of the one nearly always involves the other.

The larger question regarding peace prospects for the Sudan concerns whether conditions for peace are improving and, if so, what a solution to the conflict is likely to entail. This calls for a closer look at the causes of the problem, the current positions of the parties on the issues involved, and the options available for their resolution.

The conflict in the Sudan has evolved over the decades to a stage at which the parties are closer to an understanding on the issues that divide them yet further apart in their positions. They recognize that at the core of the civil war are disparities in the sharing of power, national wealth, and development opportunities, especially between, on the one hand, the Arab-Islamic North and, on the other, the African animist–Christian regions of the South and the largely Muslim but negroid Nuba of the Southwest. They generally agree that a redistribution of power and resources is urgently needed.

Indeed, although no consensus exists on precise solutions to the contentious problems of political and economic disparities, some broad proposals for decentralization and regional development strategies have been advanced. The insurgents have moved away from the separatist approach adopted by the Southern Sudan Liberation Movement during the first civil war, which ended in 1972. The Sudan People's Liberation Movement has embraced instead the creation of a "new Sudan," with no discrimination on the basis of race, religion, culture, or gender. At the same time, seemingly unbridgeable differences of identity appear to have emerged that are now militating against the unity of the country. The movement's call for a "new Sudan" that will remain united and at the same time fit the idealistic vision of the country is losing credibility, which makes the search for alternative solutions imperative.

The picture is complicated, however, by the split within the movement led by three SPLA commanders, Riek Machar, Lam Akol, and Gordon Kong, protesting alleged concentration of power by John Garang and human rights violations in the movement and calling for separation for the South. Paradoxically, the rebellious commanders have found themselves drawn closer to the government in a tactical alliance against the mainstream movement. This internal dissension has also generated intertribal tensions and violent conflicts, especially between the Nuer (the tribe of Riek Machar) and the Dinka, leading to the loss of thousands of lives on both sides. The emergence of a civil war within the civil war has further complicated the already difficult tasks of agencies. Combined with the SPLA's loss of its most important base of support in Africa because of the political changes in Ethiopia, the government's massive campaign during the dry season offensive of 1992 represents a significant setback for the movement.

Whatever shifts occur in the balance of power, neither side can achieve a decisive military victory in the long run. Some mutually agreed-upon solution will have to be negotiated sooner or later. Nor can the country afford to wait much longer for the resolution of the conflict, which is long overdue. The Sudan and its people have suffered too much for far too long. A resolution is also in the interest of Arab-African and Muslim-Christian relations on the continent and elsewhere in the world.

Following developments in other countries of the Horn, perhaps enduring solutions can be deferred while interim arrangements bring a semblance of peace and security to the Sudan. Ideally, the broad outlines of such arrangements should be agreed upon by the parties. For example, an agreement could confer upon the insurgents administrative control and responsibility for rehabilitation and development of the South during an interim period of specified duration, after which the larger political and constitutional issues would be addressed.

Recent developments seem to indicate a convergence of southern opinion toward easing the utopian view of a "new Sudan," which appears to have served the SPLM-SPLA well thus far. The reemerging trend is to realize that while unity is a desirable objective, it cannot

be an end in itself or justification for continuing suffering and destruction of life and property. Voices within the SPLM-SPLA, high-
lighted by the breakaway factions, have recently articulated the quest
for alternative solutions favoring a separatist agenda.

A group of southern Sudanese politicians, intellectuals, scholars,
and statesmen that met in Ireland in late 1991 adopted a declaration
based on the conclusion that the South should confront the North
with realistic alternatives rather than endlessly pursue an ideal goal
that appears extremely difficult to attain in the foreseeable future.
The three alternatives are redefining the national identity along lines
that assure the South equitable treatment; formulating a national
framework in which the two sets of people can coexist in nominal
unity, sharing vital common services but otherwise determining their
destinies independently; or partitioning the country.[6] At about the
same time, a meeting of SPLA commanders amended the movement's
manifesto, redefining the goals of the struggle to provide for self-
determination as an alternative to a united Sudan.

Future negotiations and mediation efforts should be based on these
principles and alternatives. It is difficult to see how even the government in Khartoum could question the principles, even though views
on the various options might differ. If the warring parties continue
to move further apart, however, and are determined to fight out their
differences on the battlefield, they should be held by the international
community at least to the standards of protecting civilian life that
were observed during the heyday of Lifeline.

CONCLUDING REFLECTIONS

Taken together, the emergencies in the Sudan during the past decade
provide a spectrum of experience that may inform efforts to avoid
such emergencies and to prepare for and mount future relief operations. These persisting emergencies confront the country and the
international community with potential tragedies of exceptional magnitude. The world's response provides an opportunity to implement
some of the lessons learned from relief efforts of the past decade.

Rising moral expectations that now influence international responses to such tragedies and the increasing globalization of humanitarian action mean that suffering which might have been ignored in

the past can no longer be tolerated today. Commensurate with the awakening of the world's conscience is a rise in the standards to which governments and those vying with them for political authority are held accountable for the suffering of people under their control. Those who seek to provide humanitarian relief are also subject to higher expectations.

The challenges are thus to hold political authorities accountable and to render assistance, to the extent that the authorities are incapable of providing it themselves. Maximizing the accountability of local authorities and enlisting their contribution to remedies must be a central issue for the future agenda of emergency operations. The fact that the host political authorities may no longer have the final word puts increasing pressure on the international community itself to devise and implement more effective and creative assistance and protection strategies.

The character of individual humanitarian relief operations—in the Sudan, in Iraq, and elsewhere—makes for a certain inconsistency and unevenness. The concern for international peace and security that led the Security Council to authorize humanitarian intervention in Iraq may also become a more active force when human lives and values are on the line in less publicized emergencies elsewhere. Speeding the evolution of a universal system of humanitarian action deserves to proceed on an urgent basis before additional lives are lost.

Recent experiences demonstrate that the international public, once aroused, can indeed be an effective force in counteracting threats to humanity. The world is now witnessing an upsurge of migrations by large numbers of people fleeing intolerable circumstances, whether political, economic, environmental, or social in nature. Whatever barriers are thrown up at national borders, as the suffering increases so does the likelihood of penetrating them by one means or another. Conversely, the creation of conditions conducive to security, stability, prosperity, and justice throughout the world can only result in the collective good of humanity at large.

The world should adopt a more vigorous humanitarian agenda, not only on moral grounds but also as a matter of enlightened self-interest. Where governments fail to fulfill their humanitarian responsibilities to their citizens, the human family should assert itself, with or without the support of the governments concerned. The experiences of the Sudan and, more dramatically, of Iraq suggest that a more assertive humanitarianism is no longer a distant dream but an objective capable of realization. On the other hand, failure to seize the opportunity, maintain the momentum, and move affirmatively to institutionalize improved arrangements for global responses might mark a return to the passivity of bygone days, much to the detriment of global security and well-being.

Appendix A

Persons Consulted for Office of Emergency Operations in Africa Evaluation

Sudanese Government Authorities

Khalid Affan
Hassan Atiya
Omar Hassan Ahmed al-Bashir
Mohamed Omer Beshir
Taha El Beshir
Gizouli Dafalla
Ibrahim Diraige
Hassan El Hilla
Yusuf Bekhiet Idris
Yusry Mohamed Jabr
Ibrahim El Kurdawi
Yusuf Lutfi
Sadiq al-Mahdi
Bona Malwal
Mohamed El Amin Abdel
    Rahman
Mahgoub Mohamed Salih
Abul-Gassim Seifeldin
Tawfig Shawgi
Hassan El Turabi
Ahmed Ibrahim Yusuf
Karin Abu-Zeid

United Nations System

United Nations
Bradford Morse
Maurice Strong
Keith Walton

UN Development Program
Garth Ap-Rees
Arthur Brown

Djbril Diallo
Arthur Holcombe
Charles LaMunière
Wally N'Dow
Jan van Eyndhoven
Winston Prattley
Edward Wattez

UN Emergency Operations for the Sudan
Bill Blacking
Dr. Deria
Allen Jones
Winston Prattley

UN High Commission for Refugees
Pierre Bertrand
Walter Koisser

UNICEF
Samir Basta

Office of Emergency Operations in Africa
Pierre Bertrand
Michael Cutajar
Djbril Diallo
Jane Jacqz
Salim Lone
Wally N'Dow
Edward Wattez
Michael Wickens

World Food Program
Marianne Nolte
Tekle Tomlinson
Aziz Saleh

Intergovernmental/ Governmental Organizations

George Gwyne, *European Community*
Hunter Farnham, *U.S. Agency for International Development*
David Martella, *U.S. Agency for International Development*

Nongovernmental Organizations

Mohammed A. El Asi, *Islamic African Relief Agency*
Abdullah Suleiman al-Awad, *Islamic African Relief Agency*
Arne Bergstrom, *World Vision*
Ms. Conroy, *Concern*
Mark Duffield, *Oxfam–UK*
James Firebrace, *War on Want*
Arild Jacobsen, *Norwegian Church Aid*
Penny Jenden, *Band Aid*
Colonel Hugh Mackay, *Save the Children–UK*
Emile Steinkraus, *CARE*

Appendix B
Persons Consulted for Operation Lifeline Sudan Case Study

Sudan Political Authorities

Sudan Government
Omar Hassan Ahmed al-Bashir
Pio Yukwan Deng
Dr. Abdalla Ahmed Abdalla
Dr. Abdul Hamid Latif
Ibrahim Abu Ouf
Nick Roberts

Sudan People's Liberation Movement
Ashewil M. Banggol
James Duku
Majok Akop Kuol
Commander Riak Macar
Kuol Manyang
Achol Marial
Pierre Ohure

United Nations System

United Nations
Abdulrahim A. Farah
F. T. Liu

Operation Lifeline Sudan
Hassmi Choka
Nils Enqvist
Julio Delgado Idarraga
Carlton James
Peter Jobber
Michelle John
Marcel R. LeCours
Robert McCarthy
Thomas McKnight
Myint Maung
Ruth Oloo

Vincent E. O'Reilly
Detlev Palm
Mohammed Parvez
Adrian Pintos
Babu Hailie Selassie
Willem Smit
Alastair Smith-Villers
Patta Smith-Villers
Humphrey Were

UN Development Program
Robert H. Brandstetter
Jane Wilder Jacqz
Randolph C. Kent
Basem Khader
Joana Merlin-Scholtes
Michael J. Priestley
Peter Schumann
W. Bryan Wannop

UNICEF
James P. Grant
Ulf Kristofferrson
Charles LaMunière
Marjorie Newman-Black
Farid Rahman

World Food Program
Khalid Adly
Robert C. Chase
Anis Haider
James C. Ingram
Per Iversen
Jean-Pierre Nastorg
Charles D. Paolillo
Bislow W. Parajuli
Joseph Scalise

D. John Shaw
Maas Van den Top

Other Governments

Canada
Francois Arsenault
Larry Bennett
Jean-Pierre Bolduc
Richard Chappell
Debbie Davis
Ute Gerbrandt
Frank Gillis
W. D. Rolston

Denmark
Erik Fil
Birgitte Thygesen

Kenya
Bethuel Kiplagat

Kuwait
Abdalla al-Suraya

Netherlands
Martin Koper
Hans Nieman

Sweden
Karl Lostelius

United Kingdom
John Beaven
David B. G. Bell
Hamish S. T. C. Daniel

United States
Norman Anderson
Elizabeth Bassan
Jack Davison
Hunter Farnham
William Garvelink
Michael Harvey
Joseph Gettier
Fritz Gilbert
Lowell Lynch

Dayton Maxwell
Andrew Natsios
Julia Taft

Intergovernmental Organizations

European Community
Heather Elkins
Robert Baldwin
Brian Kelly
Asger Pilegaard
Gary Quince
Elisabeth Tison

Organization of African Unity
M. T. Mapuranga

Nongovernmental Organizations

Africa Watch (London)
Alex De Waal

All Africa Conference of Churches (Nairobi)
Jose Chipenda
Harold Miller

Africa Faith and Justice Network (Nairobi)
Sister Fredericka Jacob, NDM

Africa Medical and Research Foundation (Nairobi)
Jayne Mutonga
Dr. Philip Rees

Association of Christian Resource Organizations Serving Sudan (Nairobi)
Dan Kelly
Russ Noble
Clement L. Wai-Wai

Bread for the World (Washington, D.C.)
Sharon Pauling

*Canadian Council for
International Cooperation
(Ottawa)*
Tim Brodhead
Tim Draman
Ian Filewood

Catholic Diocese of Torit
Bishop Taban Paride

*Catholic Fund for Overseas
Development (London)*
Michael Medley
Robert Rees

Catholic Relief Services
Nyambura Githangui
Robert T. Quinlan
Peter Shiras
Berhe Tewolde

Church World Service (Nairobi)
Virginia Cook
Caleb Kahuthia

*Development Group for
Alternative Policies (Washington,
D.C.)*
Gayle Smith

Dutch Interchurch Aid (Utrecht)
Jacques Willemse

*German Emergency Doctors
(Nairobi)*
Eva Grozinger
A. J. van der Perk

Human Rights Watch
Holly J. Burkhalter

INTERAID (Nairobi)
Julia Stewart

*International Catholic Migration
Commission (Geneva)*
Eugene Birrer
Andre Van Chau

*International Committee for the
Red Cross*
Dominique Buff
Pierre Gassman
Harald Schmid de Gruneck
Fred Isler
Andreas Lendorff
Vincent Nicod

*International Council of Voluntary
Agencies (Geneva)*
Tony Kozlowski
Jean-Pierre de Warlincourt

*International Rescue Committee
(Nairobi)*
Colette Byrne
Scott Portman
Ann Zimmerman

*Islamic African Relief Agency
(Khartoum)*
Abdalla Suliman El Awad
Gazuli Dafalla
Ali Tamin Fartak

*League of Red Cross and Red
Crescent Societies*
John Lloyd III
Bruce Miller
Ibrahim Osman

*Licross/Volags Steering Committee
for Disasters (Geneva)*
Robert J. B. Rossborough

Lutheran World Federation
Johan Balslev
Robert G. Koepp
Kaanaeli Makundi
Admasu Simeso

Lutheran World Relief
Sigurd Hansen
Norman E. Barth

**Maryknoll Fathers & Brothers
(Nairobi)**
Carroll Houle

**MEDIC (Comité Internationale
Médicale pour l'Urgence et
Developpement)**
Bruce Pike

**Médicins sans Frontières–Holland
(Nairobi)**
Johan Hesselink
Kees Posthuma

**Médicins sans Frontières–France
(Nairobi)**
Jean-Christophe Adrian

**Mennonite Central Committee
(Nairobi)**
William Reimer

**Missionary Aviation Fellowship
(Nairobi)**
Doug Wakeling

**National Council of Churches of
Kenya (Nairobi)**
Samuel Kobia

Norwegian Church Aid (Nairobi)
Svein Tore Rode-Christoffersen
George Waweru

Norwegian People's Aid (Nairobi)
Sharif Egal
Egil Hagen
Abdi Hassan

Oxfam–UK
David De Pury
Richard Graham

Jane Green
Anthony Nedley
Margaret Mudogo

Refugee Policy Group
Jacques Cuenod
Susan Forbes
Dennis Gallagher

Save the Children–UK
Ben Foote

Sudanaid (Khartoum)
Asma Dallalah

**Sudanese Red Crescent Society
(Khartoum)**
Ahmed Adam Gizo

**Sudan Council of Churches
(Khartoum)**
Ezekiel Kutjok

**U.S. Committee for Refugees
(Washington)**
Roger Winter

**World Alliance of YMCAs
(Geneva)**
Frank Kiehne
Joel Kinagwi

**World Council of Churches
(Geneva)**
Nico Keulemans
Melaku Kifle
Abel Mbilinyi

World Vision International
Leo Ballard
Russell Kerr
H. Dwight Swartzendruber

Media

John Gachie, *The Nation* (Nairobi)

Lucy Hannan, British Broadcasting
Corporation (Nairobi)
Charles Kulundu, *Kenya Times*
(Nairobi)
Edmund Kwena, *Kenya Times*
(Nairobi)
Gillian Lusk, *Africa Confidential*
(London)
Jim Malone, *Voice of America*
(Nairobi)
Bona Malwal, *The Sudan Times*
(Khartoum, now banned)
Philip Ochieng, *Kenya Times*
(Nairobi)
Julian Ozanne, *Financial Times*
(Nairobi)

Jane Perlez, *New York Times*
(Nairobi)

Others

Gary Ackerman, U.S. Congress
Joseph Beraki, relief worker
Federick C. Cuny, private
consultant, U.S.
Barbara Hendrie, private
consultant, U.K.
David Melvill, private consultant,
Canada
Michael Myers, U.S. congressional
staff

Appendix C
Contributing Agencies

The following agencies have supported the Operation Lifeline Sudan Case Study with cash and/or in-kind contributions:

Church World Service
The Institute for International Studies, Brown University
The International Council of Voluntary Agencies
The Lutheran World Federation
Lutheran World Relief
The Mennonite Central Committee
The Netherlands International Development Agency
The Refugee Policy Group
Sudan working group/Canadian Council for International
    Co-operation
The Swedish International Development Authority
The United Nations Children's Fund
The United Nations Development Programme
The United Nations World Food Programme

Notes

INTRODUCTION

1. The complete findings are available in two publications: Larry Minear, *Humanitarianism under Siege: A Critical Review of Operation Lifeline Sudan* (Trenton, N.J.: Red Sea Press, 1991); and Larry Minear and others, *A Critical Review of Operation Lifeline Sudan: A Report to the Aid Agencies* (Washington: Refugee Policy Group, 1990).

CHAPTER 1

1. Mohamed Omer Beshir, *The Southern Sudan: Background to Conflict* (London: C. Hurst and Company, 1968), pp. 1–2.

2. Robert O. Collins, "The Big Ditch: The Jonglei Canal Scheme," in M. W. Daly, *Modernization of the Sudan* (New York: Lilian Barber Press, 1985), p. 135.

3. Interview by Khalid Mustafa Medani, Cairo, Egypt, August 1991.

4. See Mansour Khalid, *The Government They Deserve: The Role of the Elite in Sudan's Political Evolution* (London and New York: Kegan Paul, 1990), appendix.

5. Abdalla A. Abdalla, "Importance of Agriculture and Agricultural Research in Sub-Saharan Africa," Remarks to the Sudan Focus Conference, Washington, June 6, 1991.

6. Quoted in Larry Minear, *Humanitarianism under Siege: A Critical Review of Operation Lifeline Sudan* (Trenton, N.J.: Red Sea Press, 1991), p. 21. See chapter 1 of that book for a further discussion of the situation in the Sudan and sub-Saharan Africa in the 1980s.

7. For an elaboration of the effects of war on Sudanese society and economy, see Nigel Twose and Benjamin Pogrund, eds., *War Wounds: Development Costs of Conflict in Southern Sudan* (London: Panos Institute, 1988).

8. Alex de Waal, *Famine That Kills: Darfur, Sudan, 1984–1985* (Oxford: Clarendon Press, 1989), p. 75.

9. "The Bellagio Declaration: Overcoming Hunger in the 1990s," *Food Policy*, August 1990.

10. Abdalla, "Importance of Agriculture."

11. De Waal, *Famine That Kills*, p. 196.

12. Quoted in Minear, *Humanitarianism under Siege*, p. 39.

13. Ibid., p. 65.

CHAPTER 2

1. Nick Cater, *Sudan: The Roots of Famine* (Oxford: Oxfam, 1986), p. 1.

2. Ibid., p. 4.

3. General Assembly, *Critical Economic Situation in Africa, Report of the Secretary General*, A/41/683 (United Nations, October 1986), p. 2.

4. Ibid., p. 2.

5. Ibid., p. 6.

6. Ibid., p. 7.

7. United Nations Office of Emergency Operations in Africa, Africa Emergency, *Facts* (February 1985).

8. Anders Forsse, "The United Nations and the Emergency in the Sudan: An Evaluation," unpublished, 1986, p. 11.

9. Ibid., p. 27.

10. For background on the establishment of the Office for Emergency Operations in Africa and its functioning, see Update of the Secretary General to the General Assembly, A/40/372, Adds. 1-E/1985/104, Add. 1 & 2, and A/41/683/1986 on "Critical Economic Situations in Africa."

11. Information furnished by the deputy executive coordinator, Charles LaMunière.

12. The companion evaluation on OEOA work in Ethiopia cites similar UNDRO shortcomings there but recommends reforming and strengthening it to be more effective in the future.

13. Forsse, "United Nations and the Emergency," p. 3.

14. Ibid., p. 6.

15. Ibid., p. 40.

16. "Emergency-Development Linkages: Responding to Africa's Development Crisis," A Report to the Director General for Development and International Cooperation by an informal group of UN officials (December 3, 1985).

17. Ibid., pp. 20, 22.

CHAPTER 3

1. For a more detailed account, see Larry Minear, *Humanitarianism under Siege: A Critical Review of Operation Lifeline Sudan* (Trenton, N.J.: Red Sea Press,

1991), p. 12; and Africa Watch, *Sudan: A Human Rights Disaster* (New York and Washington: The Africa Watch Committee, 1990), pp. 101–37.

2. Per Janvid, "Statement to the Economic and Social Council concerning Implementation of Emergency and Relief Operations in the Sudan, Including Operation Lifeline Sudan," pp. 1–3.

3. U.S. Agency for International Development, "Southern Sudan Assessment: Final Report," April 21, 1991–May 31, 1991, pp. 1–2.

4. U.S. Agency for International Development, "Situation Report 47" (May 14, 1991), p. 2.

5. Minear, *Humanitarian under Siege*, p. 73, chap. 3, and appendix B.

6. Ibid., p. 101.

7. Alex de Waal, "An Approach to Famine and Human Rights," unpublished.

8. For an elaboration of these issues, see Francis M. Deng, "Sudan's Struggle to Become One Nation," *Christian Science Monitor*, February 1, 1990, p. 19.

9. Janvid, "Statement to the Economic and Social Council," p. 11.

10. Embassy of the Republic of the Sudan, "Sudan Responds to the Needs of the Ethiopian Refugees," Press Release, Washington, June 17, 1991, p. 1.

11. Minear, *Humanitarianism under Siege*, pp. 59–60.

12. Ibid., p. 57.

13. Anders Forsse, "The United Nations and the Emergency in the Sudan: An Evaluation," unpublished, 1986, pp. 13–14.

14. Minear, *Humanitarianism under Siege*, chap. 5.

15. Ibid., pp. 134–35.

16. Ibid., p. 130.

17. Ibid., p. 131.

18. Ibid., p. 136.

19. Ibid., p. 140.

20. Ibid., p. 137.

21. Ibid., p. 137.

22. Ibid., pp. 92, 127.

23. Ibid., p. 59.

24. Forsse, "United Nations and the Emergency," p. 26.

25. Sadako Ogata, "Refugees in the 1990s: Changing Reality, Changing Responses," lecture at Georgetown University, June 25, 1991, p. 9.

26. Minear, *Humanitarianism under Siege*, pp. 108–09.

27. Ibid., p. 111.

28. Ibid., p. 48.

29. Ibid., p. 114.

30. For a more detailed discussion of coordination and related recommendations, see Larry Minear and others, *A Critical Review of Operation Lifeline*

Sudan: A Report to the Aid Agencies (Washington: Refugee Policy Group, 1990), pp. 17–23, 31–34, 40–43, 46, 48–49.

31. Minear, *Humanitarianism under Siege*, p. 39.

32. UNICEF Emergency Programs, "Update on Operation Lifeline Sudan," July 29, 1991, p. 2.

33. A September 1991 census placed the population of Juba, including people displaced from surrounding areas, at 316,337. "Though the number of displaced persons was less than had been assumed, the nutritional status of resident townspeople is declining seriously." U.N. Situation Report 1, Special Program for the Horn of Africa (October 1, 1991), p. 44.

34. Ibid., p. 37.

35. U.S. Agency for International Development, "Southern Sudan Assessment," pp. 2–3.

36. The UN Situation Report (October 1, 1991) observes that "people displaced by the conflict in both the eastern and western parts of Equatoria lack sufficient food; and further north in Jonglei and Upper Nile state, flooded roads have made food aid deliveries almost impossible." p. 5.

37. U.S. Agency for International Development Situation Report 50 (August 9, 1991), p. 5.

38. Minear, *Humanitarianism under Siege*, p. 33.

CHAPTER 4

1. The Thomas J. Watson Jr. Institute for International Studies of Brown University and the Refugee Policy Group of Washington, D.C., are engaged in a research project during 1991–93, Humanitarianism and War: Learning the Lessons of Recent Armed Conflicts. Its funding by UN agencies, governments, and NGOs suggests an interest throughout the international aid community in reflecting on recent experiences within the Sudan and beyond.

2. For a more extended discussion of the changing international ethos, see Larry Minear, "Humanitarian Intervention in a New World Order," Overseas Development Council, Washington, 1992.

3. Anders Forsse, "The United Nations and the Emergency in the Sudan: An Evaluation," unpublished, 1986, p. 23.

4. Ibid., p. 27.

5. For example, the groups involved in the project described in note 1 plan to publish in late 1992 a manual of principles and policy guidelines for aid practioners. The Federation of Red Cross and Red Crescent Societies is working on a similar code for NGOs.

6. The proposal was first made to Global Partners, a private international

team concerned with global issues of security, development, and the environment at their annual meeting in New York City on November 10, 1988. It was subsequently presented to the Horn Project of the Conrad Grebel College consultation in Waterloo, Canada. See Menno Wiebe, ed., *Conflict Resolution in the Horn of Africa: Envisioning Alternative Futures*, Horn of Africa Project Consultation, November 24–27, 1988 (Waterloo, Canada: Horn of Africa Project, Conrad Grebel College, University of Waterloo, October 1989), pp. 127–30.

7. The Adare Declaration of September 8, 1991.

Selected Bibliography

Abdin, Hasan. *Early Sudanese Nationalism, 1919–1925*. Khartoum: Khartoum University Press, 1985.

Adams, Barbara, and Marina Lent. *Accounting for Africa at the United Nations: A Guide for NGOs*. Philadelphia, Pa.: American Friends Service Committee, 1988.

Ahmed, Abel Ghaffar Mohamed, and Gunnar M. Sorbo, eds. *Management of the Crisis in the Sudan: Proceedings of the Bergen Forum, 23–24 February, 1989*. Bergen, Norway: University of Bergen, 1989.

Africa Watch. *Sudan: A Human Rights Disaster*. New York and Washington, D.C.: The Africa Watch Committee, 1990.

Alier, Abel. *Southern Sudan: Too Many Agreements Dishonoured*. Exeter: Ithaca Press, 1990.

An-Na'im, Abdullahi Ahmed, and Francis M. Deng, eds. *Human Rights in Africa: Cross-Cultural Perspectives*. Washington, D.C.: Brookings Institution, 1990.

Article 19 [The International Centre on Censorship]. *Starving in Silence: A Report on Famine and Censorship*. London: Article 19, 1990.

Beshir, Mohamed Omer. *The Southern Sudan: Background to Conflict*. London: C. Hurst and Company, 1968.

———. *The Southern Sudan: From Conflict to Peace*. London: C. Hurst and Company, 1975.

Cater, Nick. *Sudan: The Roots of Famine*. Oxford: Oxfam, 1986.

De Waal, Alexander. *Famine That Kills: Darfur, Sudan, 1984–1985*. Oxford: Clarendon Press, 1989.

Deng, Francis Mading. *Seed of Redemption*. New York: Lilian Barber Press, 1986.

———. *The Man Called Deng Majok: A Biography of Power, Polygyny and Change*. New Haven and London: Yale University Press, 1986.

————. *Cry of the Owl*. New York: Lilian Barber Press, 1989.

Deng, Francis Mading, and Prosser Gifford, eds. *The Search for Peace in the Sudan*. Washington, D.C.: Wilson Center Press, 1987. [Containing papers presented at the Workshop held on the subject at the Wilson Center, February 16–17, 1987.]

Deng, Francis Mading, and I. William Zartman, eds. *Conflict Resolution in Africa*. Washington, D.C.: Brookings Institution, 1991.

Forsse, Anders. "The United Nations and the Emergency in the Sudan: An Evaluation." Unpublished, 1986.

Henderson, K. D. D. *Sudan Republic*. London: Ernest Benn, 1965.

Independent Commission on International Humanitarian Issues. *Famine: A Man-made Disaster*. London and Atlantic Highlands, N.J.: Zed Books, 1985.

————. *Modern Wars: The Humanitarian Challenge*. London and Atlantic Highlands, N.J.: Zed Books, 1988.

Jansson, Kurt, Michael Harris, and Angela Penrose. *The Ethiopian Famine*. London and Atlantic Highlands, N.J.: Zed Books, 1987.

Khalid, Mansour. *The Goverment They Deserve: The Role of the Elite in Sudan's Political Evolution*. London and New York: Kegan Paul International, 1990.

————, ed. *John Garang Speaks*. London and New York: Kegan Paul International, 1987.

Lusk, Gill. "The Sudan War: Death in the South." London: Catholic Fund for Overseas Development, 1987.

Malwal, Bona. *Sudan: A Second Challenge to Nationhood*. New York: Thornton Books, 1985.

Mamud, Ushari Ahmed, and Suleyman Ali Baldo. *The Dhein Massacre: Slavery in the Sudan*. Privately printed, 1987.

Mawut, Lazarus Leek. *The Southern Sudan: Why Back to Arms?* Khartoum: St. George Printing Press, 1986.

Minear, Larry. *Humanitarianism under Siege: A Critical Review of Operation Lifeline Sudan*. Trenton, N.J.: Red Sea Press, 1991.

Minear, Larry, and others. *A Critical Review of Operation Lifeline Sudan: A Report to the Aid Agencies.* Washington, D.C.: Refugee Policy Group, 1990.

Minear, Larry, and Thomas G. Weiss. "Do International Ethics Matter? Humanitarian Politics in the Sudan." *Ethics and International Affairs,* vol. 5 (1991), pp. 197–214.

The Nordic UN Project. *The United Nations in Development.* Stockholm: GOTAB, 1991.

Peace in Sudan Group. *War in Sudan: An Analysis of Conflict.* London: Peace in Sudan Group, 1990.

Rahim, Muddathir Abd al-. *Imperialism and Nationalism in the Sudan: A Study in Constitutional and Political Development.* Oxford: Clarendon Press, 1969.

Timberlake, Lloyd. *Africa in Crisis: The Causes, the Cures of Environmental Bankruptcy.* London and Washington: Earthscan, 1985.

Twose, Nigel, and Benjamin Pogrund, eds. *War Wounds: Development Costs of Conflict in Southern Sudan.* London: The Panos Institute, 1988.

Wai, Dunstan M. *The Southern Sudan: A Problem of National Integration.* London: Frank Cass, 1973.

——. *The African-Arab Conflict in the Sudan.* New York and London: Africana Publishing Company, 1981.

Wiebe, Menno, ed. *Conflict Resolution in the Horn of Africa: Envisioning Alternative Futures.* Horn of Africa Project Consultation, November 24–27, 1988. Waterloo, Canada: Horn of Africa Project, Conrad Grebel College, University of Waterloo, October 1989.

Weiss, Thomas G., ed. *Humanitarian Emergencies and Military Help in Africa.* London: Macmillan, 1990.

Index

Abdalla, Abdalla A., 22, 31, 98, 99–100
Abuom, Tabyiegen Agnes, 5
Abu Ouf, 36
Abyei, 15, 16
Addis Ababa Agreement of 1972, 17
Africa Emergency Response System, 57
African Emergency Task Force, 57
African Medical and Research Foundation, 105
Agency for International Development (AID), U.S.: assessment of food needs and relief by, 87–88, 108, 114; conflicts with UNEOS on food relief, 61–62; and coordination of food relief, 62, 71; data surveys, 51, 52, 89; Famine Early Warning System, 89; private sector favored for food relief, 62, 69–70; response to famine, 40, 41, 46
Agriculture: breakdown as early signs of famine, 38–39, 46; colonialism, 22; declining food production, 22–23; development aid for, 17–18, 123
Airlift of food relief, 70–71; to Juba, 111–13
Akol, Lam, 133
Amnesty International, 101
Anya-Nya, 17
Arab Authority for Agricultural Development, 17

Arab-Israeli Six-Day War of 1967, 17
Arabization and Islamization process, 14–15, 17; under Nimeiri, 18–19, 92
Arab-Muslim ethnic group in the Sudan, 3, 14–15, 131
Arkell-Talab Company, 62, 69
Assistance Médicale Internationale, 105
Association of Christian Resource Organizations Serving Sudan (ACROSS), 93

Band Aid, 71, 80
Bashir, Omar Hassan Ahmed al-, 85
Beavan, John, 89
Bedri, Ibrahim, 21
Beja region, 14
Blue Nile River, 12, 44
Boutros-Ghali, Boutros, 8
British rule in Sudan, 16, 51
Brown, Bob, 62

Camp David accords, 18, 47
Canada as donor nation, 42, 63, 102
CARE, 63
Carter, Nick, 38–39
Chad, refugees from, 40, 49
Chole, Eshetu, 5
Civil war in the Sudan, 19, 23–24, 83–84; corridors of tranquility in, 84, 85, 98, 99, 110; costs, 23; food relief as factor in

continuance, 36, 98–100;
religious factors, 92–93. *See also*
Famine in the Sudan, conflict-
related
Cohen, Herman, 113, 117
Colonialism and
underdevelopment, 22
Combined Agencies Relief Team
(CART), 112
Comité Internationale Médicale
pour l'Urgence et
Developpement, 105
Commission for Relief and
Rehabilitation, 54
Context of food relief, 32, 33–35;
in conflict-related famine, 97–
104; in drought-related famine,
50–54; endemic causes of famine
and, 33; and future of food
relief, 121–22; information about
famine relief, 42, 51–54
Coordination of food relief, 35; in
conflict-related famine, 104–11;
in drought-related famine, 54–
66; and future of food relief,
122–23
Corridors of tranquility, 84, 85, 98,
99, 110
Costs of food relief, 35, 63–65, 122

Dafalla, Gazouli, 44, 76–77, 100
Dahab, Abdel Rahman Siwar al-,
44
Darfur, 11, 28; categorization of
famine in, 24–25; early signs of
famine, 39, 45; extent of famine,
43–44, 52; food aid for, 54, 63,
73; pleas for famine aid, 48–49
Darfur Relief Committee, 54
Demographics. *See* Ethnicity and
regionalism in the Sudan
Deng, Francis M., 3, 131
Dependency versus self-reliance as
issue in food relief, 66, 71–74,
111, 123

Desertification, 39, 46
Development in the Sudan:
foreign aid, 17–18, 31, 34;
human rights and, 103–04;
impact of emergency food aid
on long-term processes, 50–51;
impact of food relief activities,
101–04; inadequate funding, 78–
80; nongovernmental
organizations' role, 80–82;
relationship of food relief to
rehabilitation, 74–82
Dinka tribe, 15, 24, 131, 133
Diraige, Ahmad Ibrahim, 48
Disease, famine-related, 39, 45,
114, 115
Donor nations, 17; emphasis on
emergency food relief only, 42;
role in food relief coordination,
59, 63–64, 122–23; sovereignty
issues, 108
Drought. *See* Famine in the
Sudan, drought-related
Drought and Desertification
Commission, 54

Eastern Sudan, 16, 39, 49, 52
Economy, Sudan's national, 17,
19–20, 23
El Fashir, 40–41, 52, 54, 72
Eliasson, Jan, 8
Emergency Operations Group, 57
Enclaves, humanitarian, 131–32
Environmental degradation, 33,
39, 46
Ethiopia: food relief, 59–60, 65–66;
long-term development and
food relief, 75; war and famine,
41, 43, 45–46, 53, 116–17
Ethiopian refugees, 3, 40, 43, 49,
94, 117–18
Ethnicity and regionalism in the
Sudan, 13–16; Arabization and
Islamization process, 14–15, 18–
19; as factor in famine, 3, 16,

20–21, 44; forced relocations based on, 26–27; religion, famine food relief, and, 92–93
European Community as donor of food relief, 42, 63, 70
Evaluation of food relief. *See* Results of food relief
External nature of food relief, 32–33; in conflict-related famine, 89–97; in drought-related famine, 45–50; future of food relief, 120–21

Famine Early Warning System, AID, 89
Famine in the Sudan, 10–37; categorization, 24–25; challenges of relief operations, 31–37; early signs, 39–41, 45; ethnicity and regionalism, 3, 13–16, 20–21; geographic context, 12–13; historic episodes, 25–26; international standards of conduct and, 29–31; political context, 16–21; poverty and underdevelopment as endemic causes, 21–24; warning systems for, 89, 121
Famine in the Sudan, conflict-related, 2, 11, 83–119; context of food relief, 97–104; coordination of food relief, 104–11; external food-relief intervention, 89–97; overview of Operation Lifeline Sudan as relief, 83–89; results of food relief, 111–19
Famine in the Sudan, drought-related, 2, 10–11, 38–82; context of food relief, 50–54; coordination of food relief, 54–66; external intervention, 45–50; genesis, 38–45; results of food relief, 66–82
FAO. *See* United Nations Food

and Agriculture Organization (FAO)
Food Aid National Administration (FANA), 55
Food procurement, indigenous capabilities of, 66–69; alternative procurement methods, 39, 68–69; food storage, 67; need for focus on, 128–29
Food relief, 1–2, 120–36; assessing needs in conflict situation, 109; balance and proportionality needed, 127–28; concluding reflections, 134–36; costs, 35, 109–10; designed to decrease vulnerability to food shortages, 30, 34; as foreign policy tool of Western nations, 31, 46–47; humanitarian values, 124–25 (*see also* Humanitarian values); as human right, 79, 84; local involvement and noninvolvement, 30, 33; national sovereignty issues, 107–08, 124; needed institutional reforms, 125–30; participation of Sudanese in decisionmaking, 74; peace prospects and effects of, 36, 98–100, 130–34; problems in perspective, 120–24; slowness of international response in providing, 67–68; studies in Sudan famines, 3–7; Sudanese ambivalence, 36–37, 47–48, 50; timeliness of studies, 7–9; transport, 13, 58, 62, 69–71. *See also* Context of food relief; Coordination of food relief; External nature of food relief; Results of food relief
Food relief workers: attitudes toward government of Sudan, 102–03; expulsion, 93, 106–07; interactions with government

authorities, 104–05; lack of continuity in NGOs, 65; need for code of conduct, 127; need for training and discreet profile, 128–29; tensions between Sudanese, 95–97. *See also* Nongovernmental organizations (NGOs)
Food shortages, recurrent, 7, 10, 83
Forsse, Anders, 5

Garang, John, 34, 133; attitudes, toward famine and food relief, 116–17
Gezira region, 12
Global Information and Early Warning System, FAO, 51
Government of the Sudan: aid officials' interaction with, 104–05; attitudes and policy toward southern Sudanese, 26–27, 44; attitudes toward famine by Nimeiri regime, 26, 39–41, 45, 48–50, 54, 124; attitudes toward famine by officials, 2–3, 12, 20, 24–29, 90–91, 115–18; civil war and obstacles to food relief efforts, 84, 87–88, 90–91, 101–03, 129; emerging standards for treatment of citizens expected, 29–31; relief workers' attitudes toward, 102–03; resentments and embarrassment toward relief activities, 33, 91–92, 94–97; sovereignty issues, 107–08
Grant, James P., 99

Hailie Selasie, 46
Health, Sudan Ministry of, 54, 55
Health programs, 85–86, 101, 102
Holcombe, Arthur, 43, 59, 76
Humanitarian emergencies, need for international political review, 125–27
Humanitarian values, 124–25,

135–36; as basis for food relief, 42–43, 88, 94, 121; civil conflict and devaluation, 117–18; effect of food relief on promotion, 118–19; national sovereignty issues, 107–8; trend toward higher standards, 8–9, 29–31; undermined by religious tensions, 93
Human right(s): development linked to, 103–04; food relief and improvements in, 100–01; food relief as, 79, 84; violations, 33, 101

Immunization programs, 85–86, 102
Information on famine and food relief, 50–54; civil conflict and availability, 106; comprehension, 53–54; dissemination, 53; early warning system needs, 121; OEOA's role in gathering and disseminating, 42, 55–56, 58; scarcity, 51–53
Infrastructure and food relief, 69–71, 75. *See also* Transportation of food relief
Insurgents. *See* Sudan People's Liberation Army (SPLA)
International Committee of the Red Cross (ICRC), 91, 105
International Conference on Central American Refugees (CIREFCA), 103
International Monetary Fund, 79
International Rescue Committee, 105
Iraq, 8, 117, 124–25, 131–32
Islamic African Relief Agency, 105
Islamization of the Sudan. *See* Arabization and Islamization process

Janssen, Kurt, 59
Janvid, Per, 86–87

Juba: civil war and siege, 101–02, 111–13, 115–16; food relief, 34

Kassala, food relief for, 63
Kesha forced relocations, 26–27
Khalifa, Mohammed al-Amin, 94
Khalifa Abdullahi, 25–26
Khartoum: remoteness from rural problems, 20–21; southern Sudanese taking refuge near, 115. *See also* Government of the Sudan
Khartoum-Medani road, 13
Khartoum North-South Round Table Conference, 79
Kinyanjui, Kibiru, 36
Kong, Gordon, 133
Kordofan, 11, 15; early signs of famine, 39; extent of famine, 43–44, 52; food aid, 63
Kurds, humanitarian aid, 8, 124–25, 131–32

LaMunière, Charles, 57
Leer, civil conflict and food relief in, 114–15
Liberia, 126
Libya, 48
Lifeline. *See* Operation Lifeline Sudan
Live Aid, 80
Livestock losses and famine, 39, 40
Lutheran World Federation (LWF), 93, 111–12
Lutheran World Relief, 105

Machar, Riek, 133
Mahdi, Sadiq al-, 18, 83; interest in rural development, 77–78; overthrow, 85; as prime minister, 20, 44
Malakal, civil war in, 101–02
Malnutrition, 39, 114; determining levels, 72

Management and Logistics Team (MALT) of WFP, 63–64, 69
Manibe, Koste, 5
Media: BBC documentaries on famine, 28, 40; neglect of non-Western, 96; role in publicizing development problems, 80; role in publicizing famine, 3, 29–30, 40, 53, 128
Mengistu Haile Mariam, 18, 94, 116
Migration, famine-related internal, 39; urban growth and, 69
Minear, Larry, 5
Mohammed, Abdul, 5
Morse, Bradford, 4, 41, 56
Musa, Ohag Mohamed, 90
Muslim Brotherhood, 18, 19–20

National Islamic Front, 19, 20, 28, 117
National sovereignty issues and food relief, 107–08, 124–25
New international order, 8
New Sudan Council of Churches, 93
Ngok Dinka group, 15–16
NGOs. *See* Nongovernmental organizations (NGOs)
Nimeiri, Jaafar Mohamed, regime of, 17–20; Arabization and Islamization, 18–19; association of international food relief with, 50; attitudes and response toward famine, 26, 39–41, 45, 48–51, 54, 124; overthrow, 20, 44; ties to U.S. and Western countries, 18, 36, 46–47
Nongovernmental organizations (NGOs), 53; Combined Agencies Relief Team as consortium, 112; coordination of food relief and, 58, 63–64, 105, 122–23; indigenous Sudanese, 95–96, 105–06; lack of staff continuity

as problem, 65; national
sovereignty issues, 107–08;
religious values and expulsion
of, 93; role in long-term
development, 80–82;
transportation of food relief, 70–
71. See also Food relief workers
Northern Sudan: as drought-prone
region, 12–13; ethnic groups,
14–15; famine in (see Famine in
the Sudan, drought-related);
food aid, 63; political
domination, 16–17
Nubian region, 14
Nuer tribe, 15, 131, 133

OEOA. See Office for Emergency
Operations in Africa
OEOE. See Office for Emergency
Operations in Ethiopia
Office for Emergency Operations
in Africa (OEOA), 41–45; calls
for recreating, 7; coordination of
food relief, 55–59, 65, 122;
creation and tasks, 4–5; endemic
problems as context for efforts,
33–34; information gathering
and dissemination functions, 42,
55–56, 58, 103; principal
functions, 42; study evaluating
effectiveness, 5; UNEOS
established as arm, 43; use of
media, 80
Office for Emergency Operations
in Ethiopia (OEOE), 66
Ogata, Sadako, 103
Operation Lifeline Sudan, 11, 83–
89; context of food relief and,
97–104; coordination of food
relief and, 104–11; external
nature of food relief and, 32–33,
89–97; impartiality, 90; media
publicity, 30; results of food
relief, 111–19; role in political
conflicts, 36; study evaluating
effectiveness, 4, 5–6

Oxfam-UK: data surveys by, 51;
food relief provided by, 63
Oxfam-US, 105

Peace Havens, 131
Peace prospects, food relief
activities and, 36, 98–100, 130–
34
Population growth, 23
Poverty: as cause of famine, 21–
24; as context of food relief, 33–
35
Prattley, Winston, 59–63, 69
Priestley, Michael, 59, 107, 108

Qadhafi, Muammar, 18

Railroad system in the Sudan, 13,
58, 62, 70
Ramadan, 70
Red Cross, 91
Red Sea Hills, 11; famine, 43–44,
50; food relief, 63
Refugees: Chadian, 40, 43, 49;
definition and qualification for
UN aid, 49–50; Ethiopian, 3, 40,
43, 49, 94, 117–18; improving
emergency response to, 8–9;
Sudanese hospitality traditions
and, 94; Ugandan, 40, 49
Refugees, Sudanese: famine-
related migrations, 39, 131;
forced relocations, 26–27;
southern, relocated near
Khartoum, 115; urban migration
and, 69
Regionalism. See Ethnicity and
regionalism in the Sudan
Rehabilitation, relationship of food
relief to long-term development
and, 74–82
Relief. See Food relief
Relief and Resettlement
Commission (RRC), 95, 96, 106
Religious values as factor in civil
war and famine, 92–93

Relocations of Sudanese, famine-related, 26–27, 115
Republican Brotherhood, 19
Results of food relief, 2, 35–37; in conflict-related famine, 111–19; in drought-related famine, 66–82; future food relief, 123–24; reforms needed to improve, 125–30
Road system in the Sudan, 13, 69, 70
Road Transport Organization (RTO) of UNEOS, 64, 69
Rural areas of the Sudan: controlled by SPLA, 113–15; rehabilitation and long-term development, 77–78; scarcity of information on, 51; underdevelopment and food problems, 20–21, 41, 74

Save the Children–United Kingdom, 63, 70, 71, 81
Save the Children–United States, 63, 81
Sebstad, Jennefer, 5
Self-reliance versus dependence as issue in food relief, 66, 71–74, 111, 123
September Laws, 18–19
Shari'a laws, 18–19, 92
Shilluk tribe, 15
Smith, Gayle, 96
Social values and food relief as external intervention, 92–96
Southern Policy, British, 16
Southern Sudan, 3: ethnicity and underdevelopment, 15–16; famine in, 16, 44; government policy toward people, 26–27, 44; Nimeiri's policy toward, 17, 19; struggle for political autonomy, 17, 19, 20. *See also* Civil war in the Sudan
Southern Sudan Liberation Movement, 17

Special Political Questions, Regional Co-operation, Decolonization and Trusteeship, UN Department for, 8
SPLA. *See* Sudan People's Liberation Army
SPLM. *See* Sudan People's Liberation Movement
Stoltenberg, Thorvald, 103
Street Kids International, 105
Strong, Maurice, 4, 41, 43, 49, 56
Studies on emergency food relief, 3–7
Sudan: ambivalence toward international food relief, 36–37, 47–48, 50, 91–97; ethnicity and regionalism, 3, 13–16, 20–21; geography, 12–13; peace prospects in, 130–34; recurrent food shortages, 7, 10, 83. *See also* Development in the Sudan; Eastern Sudan; Famine in the Sudan; Northern Sudan; Southern Sudan; Western Sudan
Sudanaid, 105
Sudan Council of Churches, 93, 105
Sudanese National Commission for Refugees, 49–50
Sudan People's Liberation Army (SPLA), 19, 24, 44, 84; call for development aid by, 34; civil war and obstacles to food relief efforts, 84, 88, 90–91, 129; development activities in areas controlled by, 101–02; lack of accountability, 86; leadership's attitudes toward famine, 27, 115–17; peace prospects and internal dissension, 132–34; siege of Juba, 112–13, 115–16
Sudan People's Liberation Movement (SPLM), 19, 34, 44; peace prospects and, 132–34
Sudan Red Crescent Society, 105
Sudan Relief and Rehabilitation

Association (SRRA), 88, 95, 96, 101, 106
Sudd region, 12
Swedish Free Mission, 93

Taha, Ustadh Mahmoud Mohamed, 19
Tayeb, Omar Mohammed al-, 49
Tayeb, Tigani al-, 20
Thompson, Marcus, 107
Toposa tribe, 113
Torit region, 102
Transportation of food relief, 13, 58, 62, 69–71
Tribal administrative system, 20–21
Tribal leaders: attitudes toward accepting food relief, 93; concerns about dependency on food relief, 72–73; famine and diminished authority, 21
Tribal militias, 24, 84
Turabi, Hassan al-, 18

Uganda, refugees from, 40, 49
Underdevelopment: as cause of famine, 21–24; as context of food relief, 33–35
UNDRO. *See* United Nations Disaster Relief Organization
UNEOS. *See* United Nations Emergency Operation for the Sudan
UNICEF. *See* United Nations International Children's Emergency Fund
United Nations: coordination of food aid, 11, 41, 55–65, 82, 122; improvements in emergency response sought by, 8–9; motivations for donating food aid, 46–47; need for authority to deal with political entities, 129–30; need for international humanitarian emergency review, 125–27. *See also* Office

for Emergency Operations in Africa (OEOA)
United Nations Development Program (UNDP), 40, 43, 57; rehabilitation work emphasized by, 76; requests for food aid made to, 52
United Nations Disaster Relief Office (UNDRO), 56, 61–62
United Nations Emergency Operation for the Sudan (UNEOS), 11; conflicts with AID and UNICEF on food relief, 61–62; coordination of food relief and, 54, 59–65; establishment, 43; famine-related information disseminated by, 53; Road Transport Organization, 64, 69
United Nations Food and Agriculture Organization (FAO), 28, 46; data surveys, 52; Global Information and Early Warning System, 51; reports on famine, 52–53, 89
United Nations High Commission for Refugees (UNHCR), 49, 50, 56, 57, 129
United Nations International Children's Emergency Fund (UNICEF), 57; conflicts with UNEOS on food relief, 61; credibility as humanitarian organization, 107, 129; data surveys, 51, 52, 85
United Nations Relief Information Coordination Support Unit, 61
United Nations Security Council Resolution 688 of 1991, 124
United Nations Working Group on the Linkages between Emergency Relief and Development, 75–76
United States: as donor nation, 17, 42, 63, 122; relationship with Nimeiri regime, 17, 18, 36, 46–47; Sudanese sovereignty issues

and, 108–09. *See also* Agency for
International Development
(AID), U.S.
Urban versus rural problems in
the Sudan, 20–21, 74

Waal, Alex de, 24–25, 91
Warning systems, famine, 121
Wau, civil war in, 102
Weiss, Thomas G., 5
Western Sudan: famine, 16, 39;

food relief, 69. *See also* Darfur;
Kordofan
White Nile River, 12
World Food Program (WFP), 50,
57, 129; food aid, 63, 71;
Management and Logistics
Team (MALT), 63–64, 69;
reports on famine, 52–53, 89
World Health Organization
(WHO), data surveys, 51
World Vision International, 63, 93,
105